HOW TO RETIRE THE CHEAPSKATE WAY

ALSO BY JEFF YEAGER

Don't Throw That Away!
The Cheapskate Next Door
The Ultimate Cheapskate's Road Map to True Riches

HOW TO RETIRE
THE CHEAPSKATE WAY

The Ultimate Cheapskate's Guide
to a Better, Earlier, Happier
Retirement

JEFF YEAGER

THREE RIVERS PRESS
NEW YORK

A Word from the Author

The following book is what I call "colorized nonfiction." That means it's basically true, with the exception of any characters, passages, people, places, events, dialogue, and other stuff that I made up or at least embellished for the sole purpose of trying to keep you, the reader, from lapsing into the coma-like state commonly induced by reading books about personal finance.

Also be advised that any similarities between the cheapskates depicted in this book and you or someone you know is purely coincidental, but it may be a warning sign that your Inner Miser is trying to tell you something.

Like most books about personal finance, this one is intended as a general guide. You should seek the advice of qualified financial professionals—as well as other qualified cheapskates—about your individual financial situation and retirement plans.

Lastly, no cheapskates were killed or harmed in the writing of this book, but a few spendthrifts were accidentally waterboarded.

—JEFF YEAGER
The Ultimate Cheapskate

Copyright © 2013 by Jeffrey Yeager

All rights reserved. Published in the United States by Three Rivers Press, an imprint of the Crown Publishing Group, a division of Random House, Inc., New York.
www.crownpublishing.com

Three Rivers Press and the Tugboat design are registered trademarks of Random House, Inc.

Library of Congress Cataloging-in-Publication Data
Yeager, Jeff.
  How to retire the cheapskate way : the ultimate cheapskate's guide to a better, earlier, happier retirement / Jeff Yeager. — 1st ed.
      p. cm.
1. Retirement income—Planning. 2. Retirees—Finance, Personal.
3. Retirement. I. Title.
   HG179.Y4328 2012
   332.024'014—dc23

                            2012019928

ISBN 978-0-307-95642-2
eISBN 978-0-307-95643-9

Printed in the United States of America

Cover illustration by Scott Pollack

10 9 8 7 6 5 4 3 2 1

First Edition

To two men who have inspired me greatly:
my brother, JOEL YEAGER,
for a lifetime spent helping so many others,
and the late ROBERT B. JOHNSON,
for many of the lessons you'll read about
in the pages ahead.

"The best part of life is not just surviving, but thriving
with passion and compassion and humor and style and
generosity and kindness." Maya Angelou said it,
but I learned it from Joel and Bob.

To two men who have inspired me greatly:
my brother, JOEL YEAGER,
for a lifetime spent helping so many others,
and the late ROBERT B. JOHNSON,
for many of the lessons you'll read about
in the pages ahead.

"The best part of life is not just surviving, but thriving
with passion and compassion and humor and style and
generosity and kindness." Maya Angelou said it,
but I learned it from Joel and Bob.

Contents

HOW TO RETIRE THE CHEAPSKATE WAY

CHAPTER 1

Introduction: Who Says You Can't Afford to Retire? *Just Go Ask a Cheapskate*

Everything we'd ever read or been told about retirement planning and investing seemed to be a lie, or at least wasn't working out for us. It wasn't until we really started looking at the spending side of our finances that we began to feel like retirement was once again something within our reach . . . something we could actually control. We realized that we could simplify our lives and retire very happily on less money than we ever thought possible.

—Frugal retirees Doris and Chuck Wye

Whether your goal is to retire early or simply enjoy retirement more, this book will show you how the key to realizing your retirement dreams is more about how—and how much—you spend than it is about complicated investment schemes or even the size of your retirement nest egg.

That should be a refreshing message to many Americans today: Since the start of the Great Recession in 2008, Americans have lost more than $2 trillion in retirement savings—that's more than a third of their prerecession savings—not including the drop in the value of their homes. According to a 2011 Gallup poll, nearly 60 percent of those surveyed had changed their retirement plans because of the economic downturn. Record numbers of Americans now say they'll need to work longer than planned or believe that they may *never* be able to afford retirement.

Not so fast, say my happily retired cheapskate friends, as well as other masters of smart spending who are still working toward their dream retirements, with their retirement plans unaltered by the economic meltdown going on around them. This book contains their retirement blueprints, their tried-and-true plans for retiring the cheapskate way.

In the pages ahead, you'll meet some of my fellow "cheapskates," and I don't use that term in a pejorative sense. If you prefer, call us "frugal," "thrifty," or even just "smart consumers." In my own lexicon, being a "cheapskate" is a virtue, not a vice. It's not about being greedy or dishonest, and it's not about sacrifice or deprivation. It's all about choices—deciding what's really important in your life (particularly those things that come without a price tag) and skipping the rest. I honestly believe that most Americans—not all, but most—would be happier, and the quality of their lives would actually *increase,* if only they would spend and consume less.

So, to me, a "cheapskate" is the polar opposite of a "conspicuous consumer." Cheapskates are too self-confident—and frankly too smart—to spend money on things they don't need, and probably don't even want, just to impress others. Cheapskates believe that their time here on earth is too precious to waste it chasing after more money and more stuff than what they really need. And, as you'll see, many of them have decided they really don't "need" that much to be happy.

At age fifty-four, I've been a practicing cheapskate most of my adult life, although I've fallen off the wagon a few times along the way. Having grown up in the rural Midwest, in a family that viewed spending money as an option of last resort, I was raised in a culture that knew the value of a dollar and placed a premium on thrift and frugality. Heck, we were proud of our ability to pinch a penny until Lincoln cried. In fact, rumor has it that the Yeager family crest bears the inscription "Spartium Homo Erectus," which, of course, is Latin for "Cheapskate Who Stands on Two Feet."

We were by no means poor. But with two sets of grandparents hardened by living through the Great Depression and loving parents who taught us that many of the best things in life truly are free, I learned the value of "thriftcraft" at a young age. It's little wonder that, with my upbringing, for a career I settled in the nonprofit sector—where stretching a buck is a job requirement—and spent twenty-five years as a CEO and fund-raiser for a number of national nonprofit organizations in Washington, DC.

Because I practice what I preach when it comes to frugal living and smart money management, at the age of forty-seven I was able to "functionally retire," or—as I'll talk more about later—become "selfishly employed." Selfish employment is when you have at least enough financial security and independence to be able to do whatever the heck you want to do for a living, regardless of how much you might, or might *not*, earn from doing it. So that's when I became the Ultimate Cheapskate and started writing about money (and, specifically, spending less of it!), based on my own life experiences and the financial lessons I'd learned as a non-profit manager.

That was seven years and three books ago, and during that time I've been thinking a lot about the topic of retirement and talking with a great many of my Miser Advisers about it as well. *Miser Advisers?* Oh, those are fellow frugal folks living all around the world who keep me supplied with tips, stories, and ideas about enjoying life more by spending less—my sort of "bargain-basement brain trust." You'll meet some of them shortly.

What occurred to me was that we cheapskates have some rather different views and approaches to retirement from those of most people, just as we do on lots of things in life . . . well, at least those things involving money. While no two cheapskates are alike—nor are their visions or plans for retirement—I found in my conversations and research that many of us share certain common strategies when it comes to achieving our retirement dreams, whatever they may be. I found that there really is a "cheapskate way to retire better, earlier, and happier." Particularly in light of the impact the current economy is having on most people's retirement plans, I thought that sharing what I've learned on the topic in this book might help people gain a new, more positive perspective on their own retirements.

Because I don't write traditional personal finance books,

I always feel compelled to give readers a few words of advance warning about what to expect. As I often say: *I don't write books about how to get rich; I write books about how to get happy, perhaps with what you already have.* That seems to me to be the real key to enjoying life, particularly when it comes to enjoying retirement, when many will be living on a fixed income.

So by way of warning, if you're looking for a book about retirement investing—particularly magical ways to hatch an ostrich-size retirement nest egg overnight without working or planning for it—this isn't that book. The good news is, most books written about retirement focus almost exclusively on investing, so go pick up one of those books instead. Of course, these days, a lot of those tomes should be reclassified from nonfiction to fiction, given the experience of countless folks like Doris and Chuck Wye, who followed their advice like a rooster chasing a hen around the barnyard, and with a similar outcome. That's right, they got screwed.

No, while this book offers lots of practical advice on how it's possible to free up money you didn't think you could and thereby have more to set aside for retirement, other than a few anecdotal stories about how different cheapskates have in their own lives invested their retirement nest eggs, this is not a book about investing. This is a book about what I believe is the more important side of personal finance and retirement planning: the spending side.

Few people have the luxury of setting their own salaries, or dictating the rate of return on their investments, or knowing with any certainty that the lottery ticket they buy today is going to be the mega-million-dollar winner tomorrow. But every day, whenever we get out our wallets or open up our purses, we're controlling—or, in many instances, choosing *not* to control—the spending side of our finances. That's why "return on noninvestment" (as in "NOT SPENDING!") is ultimately a far more important and powerful concept than the incessantly discussed, debated, and written-about concept of "return on investment."

The other thing I'll warn you about up front is that I know for a fact you won't be able to relate to every cheapskate you'll meet in the pages ahead. You may even find some of them and their lifestyles, well, a little weird or off-putting. In selecting people to include in this book, I tried to purposely recruit a diverse group, people leading a wide range of lifestyles, with different backgrounds, family situations, retirement plans, and expectations, and, yes, occasionally quirky behavior.

So, while you may not see yourself in each and every person or family I mention in the book—in fact you should have yourself tested for multiple personality disorder if you do—I trust that by the end you will have at least a small epiphany: *Gee, there's someone out there just like me who is planning for or already enjoying the retirement I want, and they're doing it better than me and for much less. They're retiring the cheapskate way, and I can too!*

Tell Me What You Want, What You Really Really Want

— — — — — — — —

I guess for a long time I was like a lot of young people. I was going along in life, working at a job that for the most part was enjoyable and rewarding enough. However, as the work-week wore on, like most people, I found myself humming the words to a familiar country-and-western song more and more often—you know, "Working for the Weekend." That's when I first started to think about retirement.

I was in my mid-twenties, married to Denise—the love of my life, whom I met my senior year in college—and work-ing for a nonprofit organization in Washington, DC. I deeply supported (and still do) the mission of that organization, American Youth Hostels. It had helped shape my life since I was a teenager and taught me that travel is among the high-est forms of education and one of the richest values in life.

I loved the people I worked with, and the work itself—planning bicycle and hiking trips all around the globe for groups of young people—was as fascinating as it was some-times stressful.

There were midnight calls from frantic trip leaders to report lost group members, lost bicycles, lost passports, lost virginities, lost airline tickets, lost traveler's checks, and—in more than one case—lost trip leaders. "You're the leader. You can't be lost," I'd tell them. "Everyone else is lost. Now get on your bicycle and go find them!"

Then there were the ten angry calls from ten angry

parents and their ten angry attorneys one sweaty Monday morning in July 1981. That was the day after their thirteen- and fourteen-year-old darlings had arrived home from one of our European bike tours, all sporting freshly minted tattoos and assorted body piercings, authorized by the trip leader as their temporary legal guardian. Apparently what happens in Amsterdam doesn't stay in Amsterdam. Pass the Maalox, please.

After a few months in that job, my skin grew thicker as my stomach lining grew thinner. But the realization that I wasn't getting any younger started to weigh more and more on my mind. I started paying much greater attention to my paycheck, what little was left of it after that FICA guy took his cut.

Working in the nonprofit sector had intangible rewards for sure. But when it came to more mundane affairs like salaries, benefits, and retirement plans, you had to swallow pretty hard every other Friday when Annette from the accounting department handed you your paycheck. As the sign I posted on the bulletin board in my office cubicle read, "Working here is like peeing your pants when you're wearing a dark blue suit: You feel nice and warm all over, but nobody notices."

That really wasn't true though, and I knew it. I knew that the organization I was working for and the job I was doing were having a positive impact on the lives of thousands of young people, just as it had helped shape my own life. I knew that at least for some of them, it would truly be a life-changing experience, lasting far beyond the time it took for their tattoo removal scars to heal over.

But the thing I didn't know was how I could continue to afford to do the type of low-paying work I was drawn to, while at the same time enjoying a comfortable-if-not-luxurious life and building enough financial security so that someday Denise and I could retire. At that point, I hadn't even been able to free up enough extra funds to match my employer's modest contribution to the organization's 403(b) retirement plan, the nonprofit version of a 401(k).

One spring day I was sitting on a bench in Franklin Park across the street from the youth hostel where our offices were located. I had just chomped into the cold-cut sub I bought most every day for lunch at the New York–style deli across the street. A coworker, Bob Johnson, walked up and asked if he could join me.

I didn't know Bob well, although in the short chats we'd had while waiting in line together to use the Xerox machine, he'd impressed me as a very smart man with a keen but understated sense of humor. He was a member of the senior management team, while I was so low on the corporate ladder that I was still holding the shoes of the guys who were still holding the ladder. Even though he was only about ten years older than me, his full but prematurely gray head of hair made him seem much older, in a distinguished, philosopher-sage type of way.

After some small talk, Bob unwrapped a turkey-on-rye sandwich he'd brought from home and asked me a few questions about how I was enjoying my job and life in Washington. Sitting on that park bench next to Bob, I found myself doing something entirely out of character for me. For whatever reason, I felt I could bare my soul—and specifically my growing financial angst—to this man whom I hardly knew.

I just started to talk, and talk, and talk. Occasionally, bits of assorted lunch meats flew out of my mouth, but I just kept talking. I talked about how much I loved the organization, and how, in many ways, I'd magically found my dream job in my very first job out of college. And then I started talking about money, and my increasing worries about not being able to survive—let alone plan for the future—on the level of financial compensation an organization like the one we both worked for could realistically provide.

Bob just listened. He let me do all the talking. He let me finish my sub, as well as the bag of chips and can of Coke I'd bought to go with it.

And then, as if channeling the future Spice Girls (who at the time were still in kindergarten), Bob looked straight at me and said, "So, tell me what you want. What you really, really want out of life. That's the first step if you're serious about making a career out of this type of work, living a comfortable life on what it can pay you, and someday even retiring from it. Once you've figured that out, figuring out the money stuff really isn't that hard."

Although I didn't believe him at the time—at least the

part about "the money stuff really isn't that hard"—Bob and I instantly became best friends. Over the next few years, we would have many conversations about how to get what you really want out of life and plan for the future by being smart about using whatever financial resources you have available to you, regardless of their limitations, just as we did in our careers as nonprofit managers. Bob Johnson became my mentor in helping me to understand that it's the *spending*—far more than the *earning*—that makes the biggest difference.

And while, sadly, Bob would not himself live long enough to ever enjoy his own retirement, barely twenty-five years after we sat together for the first time on that pigeon-splattered park bench, thanks to Bob, I was able to embark on my own retirement dream. Yes, even after spending a modest-paying career doing the nonprofit work I loved. Bob was right, once you know what you really, really want, *the money stuff really isn't that hard.*

Retirement: *The Times They Are a-Changin'*

If you've thought about retirement at all in recent years, you know the news media are a-buzz with reports and surveys about how the recent recession has decimated so many Americans' retirement plans and dreams. I'm not trying to minimize the very real, very negative impact that the recession has had on most Americans' finances. Whether your financial priorities are retirement planning, affording a decent home, sending your kids to college, or just putting bread on the table, the recession has been a major kick to the money groin of most families.

It's interesting, though, when you look at a number of different surveys (all circa 2011) about the impact the recession has had on people's retirement planning and expectations. In reviewing three of those surveys in particular, I was reminded of a favorite observation of a friend of mine. He's fond of telling people (inaccurately, perhaps) that the Chinese word for "crisis" consists of the corresponding characters for "danger" and "opportunity" combined.

Whether or not my friend's Mandarin is up to snuff, or whether it's just the sake talking, it strikes me that you can interpret America's changing trends and attitudes toward retirement in the same way.

At one extreme, you have recent surveys like the Gallup poll mentioned earlier and one commissioned by the National Institute on Retirement Security, which showed that more than 75 percent of Americans feel that the average worker in the current economy cannot save enough on their own to guarantee a secure retirement. That same survey showed that 84 percent of respondents said that the current economic climate had adversely impacted their ability to achieve a secure retirement. Surveys like these clearly paint a picture of the "crisis" Americans are facing—or at least feeling—when it comes to their retirement plans.

Then there are a number of other surveys, including a

fascinating one from the SunAmerica Financial Group and Age Wave, that look more closely at how Americans are responding to the "dangers" the recent recession has posed to their retirements. In large part, the response has been a marked shift in attitudes and expectations about retirement, almost a redefining of what "retirement" means. Among older workers participating in that survey, 54 percent now say they view retirement as "an opportunity for a whole new chapter in life." When the same survey asked that question in 2001, almost two-thirds of respondents said they viewed retirement as a continuance of what life was or a winding down of life. The new retirement is one centered around continuing to be productive, making a meaningful contribution in life, and even reinventing yourself.

In light of those shifting attitudes, it's not surprising that the SunAmerica survey also showed that 65 percent of respondents said that, ideally, they would like to remain employed (at least part-time) during some or all of their traditional retirement years. Sure, for some, the decision to delay retirement or continue working part-time is not a matter of desire, but rather a financial necessity. But for a majority, it isn't: 54 percent said they wanted to continue some level of employment during their retirement years for the "stimulation and satisfaction" they get from their jobs.

And, finally, a survey intriguingly titled *The 2011 MetLife Study of the American Dream* highlights what are some of the "opportunities" emerging out of the crisis known as the Great Recession. It brings us back to the question, What do you really, really want out of life and retirement?

The MetLife study states: "Emerging trends show Americans are less concerned with material issues, and that life's traditional markers of success do not matter as much today. Rather, achieving a sense of personal fulfillment is more important toward realizing the American Dream than accumulating material wealth. This is a significant shift, as it reflects that Americans value close relationships with family and friends as more important than money, and that being content with what they have and balancing work/life issues are more important than 'living large.' Today, material possessions matter less, and personal relationships matter more."

If that's true—or at least if it's true in your own life—then I'm more certain than ever that retiring the cheapskate way is for you. Because I know for a fact that there are far more opportunities for you to enjoy retirement than there are dangers or other barriers keeping you from doing so, despite the crisis we've all just weathered. Remember, retiring the cheapskate way is not about sacrifice or deprivation. It's all about choices.

Are You Ready for a Cheapskate Intervention?

Before we head off down the road to meet some of my fellow cheapskates and learn about their tips and secrets for retiring better, earlier, and happier, one final word of warning. Well, it's actually more a word of reassurance: Even if you're new to the world of frugality, newcomers are always welcome, and we promise to be gentle in your initiation into the World of Cheaphood. Of course, from time to time, you might need a little Cheapskate Intervention. Here are some warning signs:

☞ *You might need a Cheapskate Intervention if you think that FICA is a kind of houseplant that always dies two weeks after you buy it.*

☞ *You might need a Cheapskate Intervention if you own both a riding lawn mower and a treadmill.*

☞ *You might need a Cheapskate Intervention if you think "layaway" is an island in the South Pacific.*

Okay, you get the idea, so off we go.

A LITTLE EXERCISE TO GET YOU STARTED

"It sounds simple, but it really made me think." Bruce Jackson, one of my favorite cheapskates, whom we'll visit with in Chapter 6, is telling me about an exercise he participated in many years ago that's always stuck with him.

We're having dinner on a linoleum-topped table at a pizza parlor a few blocks from his home in Lewisburg,

Pennsylvania (Bruce even bought, after a few rounds of "Two cheapskates go out for dinner . . ." jokes), and I'm having a déjà vu moment. It's a flashback to sitting on that park bench with my friend and mentor Bob Johnson. Because the exercise Bruce is recalling is ultimately about "what you really, really want" and—just as important—"what it really, really costs."

Bruce is right: it is pretty simple, but also pretty interesting. Take out a piece of paper (or several) and just start writing down everything—and I mean *everything*—you enjoy doing in life. Don't get bogged down by trying to keep it organized, or profound, or something that will ever be seen by anyone other than you. This is intended as a stream-of-consciousness exercise, not an IQ or memory test. And you don't need to finish it in one sitting; in fact, keep coming back to it later as you think of more things to add.

Now, once you've compiled your list of favorite activities, go through it and put a dollar sign next to every item on the list that costs money to do. If you really want to get fancy or if you have interests that run the gamut from "Dollar Store Cheap" to "Saks Fifth Avenue Expensive," develop your own system for using multiple dollar signs to rate the relative costs of doing different things on your list.

After you've finished, sit back and take a careful look at the whole list. It should tell you a lot about how much money you're really going to need to *enjoy* retirement. Who knows, you may even discover that there are not that many items on your list with dollar signs next to them, and that you may already be a lot closer to the level of financial independence you need to retire. That's what Bruce Jackson discovered when he made his list . . . and decided that he could happily retire at the ripe old age of thirty-nine.

KELLY AND JON NOWAK

Newlyweds, but Not Newly Frugal

Married for a mere eight weeks at the time I interviewed them, newlyweds Kelly and Jon Nowak were quick to confess that retirement and retirement planning were not top-of-mind issues for them at that precise moment. In fact, the earnest young midwestern couple were actually downright apologetic about their lack of preparedness.

Go figure. What couple in full-blown honeymoon mode aren't thinking about variable retirement annuities, 401(k) distribution regulations, and long-term care insurance? Had they lost all sense of what's truly important in life?

Both in their early thirties and marrying for the first time, the Nowaks were clearly still in that magically giddy postwedding phase—that wonderful time in life when you wake up every morning thinking, *I can't believe we're actually married!* In Kelly and Jon's case, I'm absolutely confident that they'll be saying that same thing every morning for the rest of their lives, and that the emphasis will never shift to be on the words "can't" and "actually," as it sadly does in so many marriages. You know, as in, *I* can't *believe we're* actually *married!*

Jon has worked for the past twelve years as an HVAC service technician, and Kelly has spent her career working for nonprofit agencies as an occupational therapist. Both make decent but not spectacular salaries, placing them very much in the same middle-class income bracket as the households in which they were raised. Both also participate in the retirement plans sponsored by their employers.

I first met Kelly (then Kelly Kamann) a couple of years earlier, when I interviewed her for my book *The Cheapskate Next Door: The Surprising Secrets of Americans Living Happily Below Their Means*. At the time, she'd impressed me as one of the most financially responsible young women I'd ever met. She still does. So, when I learned that a major Miser Adviser of mine was getting married, inquiring cheapskate minds wanted to know: What kind of man does a very attractive, successful, financially savvy woman like Kelly select as a worthy suitor and spouse?

"No!" Kelly and Jon say in perfect unison. My question: "Could you see yourself marrying someone who felt the opposite about money matters as you do?"

Both are equally quick to clarify that it was true love—and not shared attitudes about money—that brought them together. But after meeting on a blind date arranged by mutual friends two years earlier, the couple quickly realized that they had many important things in common, and their similar approaches to personal finances was one of them.

"It just wouldn't have worked if I'd found someone who was deeply in debt or who liked to spend a lot of money," Kelly says. "You know how I am, Jeff, and Jon feels pretty much the same way I do. Neither of us has ever lived beyond our means. That's just not how we were raised."

The only debts the young couple have are the mortgages on the homes they each own. No car loans; no personal loans; no credit card debt; no home equity loans; and no student loans (although Kelly graduated with $16,000 in student loans, which she promptly paid off within four years after graduating). And, as you might guess, they even have an ample emergency fund and other savings set aside for unexpected expenses or if they decide to make a major purchase.

On the subject of debt, it's clear that there's not even enough room to slide the couple's newly minted marriage certificate between Kelly's and Jon's shared views on the topic. "I've just never understood borrowing money for things you know you can't afford," Jon says.

The Nowaks are currently living in Kelly's small but comfortable home, and Jon is temporarily renting out his house to his brother. However, both houses are now officially up for sale, with the plan being to eventually buy a slightly larger home than either of the ones they currently own.

"We're not going to buy a huge home or a brand-new home," Kelly says. "But we do want to have enough space for children," she adds with a little blush. "We want to find a home that will work for us now, and when we have kids, and even in our old age. We want it to be a home where we can live forever," she says, as Jon nods his head in agreement.

Even though the couple's existing homes have dropped in value since they bought them—as with so many splatter victims of the bursting of the housing bubble—they both expect to walk away from the sale of their homes with enough for a healthy down payment on a new home. Between improvements they've made to their homes and, in Kelly's case, aggressively paying down a fifteen-year mortgage on her home, they've both managed to build equity *even* as the value of the homes has declined. And when the couple eventually sell their current homes and go house shopping, they plan on buying a place that they can afford on just one of their salaries alone.

As they're telling me all of this, I'm smiling a little and thinking to myself, *Here's a young couple that are apologetic for not having a formal retirement plan all laid out within the first two months of their marriage, but everything they're doing is exactly what a couple their age should be doing to someday happily retire, the cheapskate way.* They're living within— even *below*—their means. They're avoiding debt like the plague. They're contributing to their employer-sponsored retirement plans. And they're planning to buy a more modestly priced home than what a mortgage lender will likely tell them they can afford, and then stay in that home for a very long time, maybe even forever. When the Nowaks eventually sit down to pencil out an official retirement strategy (which, knowing Kelly, will be before the proofs come back from their wedding photos), pretty much everything in that plan will be things they're already doing.

When I broach the subject of having children, both Kelly and Jon talk about how they plan to raise their children in much the same way they themselves were brought up, placing a priority on spending time together as a family as opposed to simply *spending*. "There are so many things you can do with kids that are free or don't cost much," Kelly says, adding that both of their families have small cottages in the area, so the Nowaks anticipate spending plenty of family together-time there. Kelly is hopeful that by the time they do have children, she'll be able to at least cut back on the number of hours she works at her job.

Even with such similar views on money matters—or perhaps because of it—the Nowaks have already decided that managing their financial affairs as a married couple will definitely be a shared responsibility, and their funds will be combined and held jointly. "At first I thought maybe just one of us would handle it—paying the bills, balancing the checking account, and so on," Jon says. "But now I think both people in a marriage need to be involved and know what's going on with their finances. That seems like the healthiest way."

Kelly had what I consider to be a particularly insightful answer to my final question: "What money advice would you give to other newlyweds like yourselves?" Without a moment's thought, she says, "Just because you're newlyweds doesn't mean that you need to have everything new and everything right away. It's easy to get caught up in being newly married, and go hog wild, buying all new stuff. It's like nothing you owned when you were single is good enough anymore and you deserve to buy new."

Jon has a big boyish grin on his face, and I ask him what he finds so amusing. "Well, it's just that Kelly made me throw away nearly every piece of clothing I owned as soon as we got married and buy new!"

"Oh Jon!" Kelly says with a laugh. "Jeff, he dressed like a homeless man. Those old rags just had to go." Apparently there are some things in life even a frugal bride doesn't mind spending a little money on.

CHAPTER 2

Getting Your Money Priorities Straight, Cheapskate-Style

- -

"It isn't rocket science. Heck, it isn't even bicycle mechanics. I'll bet even a farm boy from Ton-tog-an-y, Ohio, can figure it out. 'Ton-tog-an-y,' is that how you say it? Isn't that an old Iroquois word for 'Where the simpletons live'?"

Bob Johnson and I are sitting on the patio of a youth hostel outside of Gimmelwald, Switzerland. It's a gorgeous fall day, and we're gazing at a view of the Swiss Alps that looks like a painting by the late Bob Ross. You know, Ross was the guy with the Afro and goatee on PBS who was famous for teaching those of us who are artistically challenged how to extract amazing landscapes out of a bare canvas, simply by "deciding where your *footy* hills live" and "building us some happy little trees" and "a happy little cloud that floats across the sky."

Bob and I are attending an international youth hostel conference, one of the few perks of our jobs, and I'm once again picking his brain about money. And he's once again poking fun about my rural upbringing and the small town where I'm from, the name of which he claims is unpronounceable and for which he's constantly coming up with different Native American interpretations of its possible meaning.

By that time I'd known Bob for about three years, and a lot of what he'd taught me about money—and getting what you really, really want out of life, even on a limited salary—was only common sense. Even by the end of our first lunch-time encounter that day in the park, he'd pointed out that if I started packing my lunch every day, as he always did, rather than buying carryout, I'd easily save enough in a year to solve at least one of my money worries: not having enough spare cash to take advantage of the modest match our employer offered through the organization's 403(b) retirement plan. From that day forward I became a brown-bag devotee like Bob and had my first dollar saved for retirement. "Ton-tog-an-y. I think that's Chippewa for 'Now that wasn't so hard, was it?'"

And it was Bob who introduced Denise and me to the idea of buying a "forever home," one we could fix up ourselves, as our finances and skills allowed, and ideally one that had some income-producing potential, like a duplex or a small attached rental unit. I think Bob was even more excited than we were when Denise and I found our forever home, complete with a small guest cottage that would make a perfect rental. He not only coached us through the home buying process ("Remember, everything, and I mean *everything*, is negotiable") but literally crawled through every square inch of the house I sometimes describe as "a proto-type of the Branch Davidian compound" just to make sure it was sound. "Ton-tog-an-y. Isn't that Sioux for 'Sure hope you know how to swing a hammer'?"

There were so many other lessons about money—both big and small—that Bob taught me over the years. But that day on the patio in Switzerland, Bob quickly, almost impatiently, drew me one of his famous back-of-a-napkin diagrams that forever changed my outlook on money. I've since expanded on his napkin sketch and dubbed it "the Cheapskate's Hierarchy of Moolah Management."

The Cheapskate's Hierarchy of Moolah Management

It's important to understand the cheapskate's mind-set for financial planning and priorities, particularly in thinking about and planning for retirement the cheapskate way. You'll find that the cheapskate's perspective on financial priorities is almost the exact opposite of how many people—including many financial pundits—view money, especially when it comes to investing.

Here's what Bob fleshed out on the napkin that day, a cheapskate's prioritization—from what's most important to what's least important—of money management.

1. **Reduce your dependency on money as much as possible, thereby reducing your need for greater cash flow. (MOST IMPORTANT)** Cheapskates place the highest priority on

spending less, not earning more. Living a "money-lite" life has three primary components:

- Differentiate between "needs" and "wants." Attempt to reduce your routine living expenses ("needs") to be no more than 50 percent of your income, and allocate no more than 20 percent to "wants," with the balance (at least 30 percent) going into savings. At a minimum, live within your means always, and live below your means whenever you can.

- Establish a "permanent standard of living" (see Chapter 3), and refuse to allow your expenses to escalate as your income grows during your working years.

- Keep debt out of your life as much as possible, and when you do take on debt (e.g., to buy a home), make paying off that debt as quickly as possible your top financial priority.* Doing so will save you one of life's largest—and least enjoyable—expenses: the cost of servicing debt. It will also help avoid nasty things like foreclosures and bankruptcy.

2. **Maintain your health, thereby preserving your ability to work and earn money as needed and reducing the chances of incurring catastrophic medical expenses.** Sure, there

---

*In terms of planning for retirement the cheapskate way, the only higher priority than paying off debt is allocating funds to qualify for any amounts your employer may be offering to match through your company's retirement plan. Otherwise, paying off debt is the top priority.

are no guarantees when it comes to maintaining good health, although a lot of people choose to do a lot of the things that significantly worsen the odds against it (see Chapter 7).

3. **Safeguard your assets (both liquid and fixed) as you obtain them.** The easiest dollar you'll ever earn is the one you've already earned and don't lose or waste. There are four aspects to this rule:

- Develop a proclivity for safe(r) investments over more risky ones. After all, if you can live comfortably on less money, you don't need to gamble so aggressively on high-risk investments. The preservation of capital becomes the overriding consideration.

- Create an individualized asset allocation plan, a plan for what types of investments make sense for you and involve whatever level of risk you can tolerate and still sleep well at night. Remember, in the very act of diversification there is, almost without exception, greater security. "Ton-tog-an-y. Isn't that Lakota for 'Don't put all your eggs in one basket'?"

- Maintain appropriate insurances to protect yourself and your assets.

- Take care of your stuff. Investing time and money to maintain the possessions you already own—from your house and car, to your wardrobe and the kids' bicycles—is one of the best investments you can make.

4. **Attempt to maximize the growth of your portfolio and other assets, as time and interest allow. (LEAST IMPORTANT)** Note that this is the lowest priority, whereas most noncheapskates view it as the highest. In fact, when you think about it, if you have sufficiently mastered the first three priorities in this hierarchy, this final one is really optional, at best.

There you have it, the Cheapskate's Hierarchy of Moolah Management. "Ton-tog-an-y. Isn't that Mohican for 'The last financial advice you'll ever really need'?"

The Importance of Living Below Your Means

In a 2009 survey I did of more than three hundred proud, self-proclaimed cheapskates for my book *The Cheapskate Next Door,* I found that, on average, the cheapskates I surveyed were spending only about 65 percent of what they earned. And this was with a survey population that spanned the income spectrum from folks earning mid-six-figure salaries to some earning so little that they could qualify for public assistance but chose not to because they were living quite comfortably on what they earned.

A majority of the two-income families I surveyed said their practice was to live on just one of their two salaries and save the other. Obviously this allowed them to bank a significant amount in savings, not just for retirement, but for their kids' college funds, unexpected emergencies, major purchases, and—yes—some occasional splurges.* The other benefit of this common cheapskate approach of living on just one income and saving the other is that it insulates the family from financial hardship in case one spouse loses a job—something a number of my cheapskate families have unfortunately experienced during the recession.

☞ *You might need a Cheapskate Intervention if you sit by the phone all day hoping that robo-caller "Rachel, from card member services" will call to help you straighten out your credit problems.*

Cheapskates have found creative ways (discussed in this book as well as in my others) to reduce their living expenses to a fraction of what most Americans spend on everything from housing, to transportation, to food, clothing, education, recreation, and just about everything else. To give you an idea of how much less they spend, here are some of the results from my 2009 cheapskate survey:

- **Housing:** 27 percent less,† in part because they're living in smaller, more comfortable homes (see Chapter 6)

---

*Cheapskates like to have fun just like everybody else . . . but they don't want to ruin the experience by going into debt to do so.
†All comparisons are based on data from the US Bureau of Labor Statistics' Consumer Expenditure Survey 2008.

and staying in them longer than typical Americans. And that 27 percent is just based on the purchase price; it does not include the astronomical lifetime savings in interest, since almost 85 percent of cheapskates plan to pay off their home mortgages early or already have done so.

- **Food:** Almost 75 percent less on meals prepared outside the home (restaurant and carryout), and nearly 40 percent less on groceries.
- **Transportation:** 42 percent less, with five out of six buying good-condition used vehicles instead of new and, on average, owning 1.8 vehicles per household as opposed to the national average of about 2.5 vehicles.
- **Clothing:** An astonishing 71 percent less! Cheapskates love to buy secondhand clothing, avoid trendy fashions that quickly go out of style, and buy quality garments that they take good care of and wear for years.
- **Entertainment/recreation:** Roughly 30 percent less, even though cheapskates enjoy their leisure time, including travel—those surveyed were twice as likely as the average American to have traveled abroad.

When it comes to retirement planning the cheapskate way, the importance of consistently living below your means throughout your life cannot be overstated. When you think about it, doing so has three powerful benefits. First, of course, it allows you to set aside money in your retirement nest egg. Second, it conditions you to live on a fixed, limited amount of money; think of it as "test-driving" your retirement lifestyle/budget. And third, by following Kelly and Jon Nowak's example and living below your means right from the very start of your working years, you're able to invest your savings in lower-risk ways, rather than being forced to gamble on riskier investments to make up for lost time.

Cheapskate Retirement Principle #1

Consistently living below your means throughout your working years is one of the most important keys to retiring better, earlier, and happier. It allows you to save for retirement, conditions you to living on a fixed budget, and lets you avoid having to gamble on risky investments to make up for lost investing time.

The Importance of Avoiding Debt and Retiring Debt-Free

How would you like to have an extra $600,000 saved for your retirement? According to a fascinating but shocking chart put together by the website CreditLoan.com, titled "The Lifetime of Debt: The Financial Journey of the Average American" (http://www.creditloan.com/infographics/a-lifetime-of-debt-the-financial-journey-of-the-average-american), that's how much the average American is now projected to pay in interest over course of his or her lifetime. It makes me nauseous even thinking about it.

Among other frightening factoids from CreditLoan.com's "The Lifetime of Debt":

- The first payment-based debt (e.g., credit card debt, a car loan, etc.) is now typically incurred by Americans while they are still in high school. Heck, when I was in high school, my *parents* didn't even have a credit card!

- The average undergraduate in college has $3,200 in credit card debt; the average graduate student has about $8,600. Only 2 percent of undergraduates have no credit history. Why isn't graduating without a credit history every bit as important as graduating with honors?

- The average college student amasses about $20,000 in student loan debt toward his or her first degree, and if they get a master's degree, that jumps to about $37,000. But that ain't nothin', because the average medical school student graduates with $113,000 in student debt (no wonder health-care costs are so high).

- The average auto loan is now for more than $30,000, a 40 percent increase in the last ten years. Two-thirds of American households now own two or more automobiles, and most Americans are driving down the road in a car they're still paying for.

- The average home mortgage is about $240,000 and is financed under a thirty-year mortgage, which means that your house ends up costing more than $580,000, including interest. Of course, most Americans buy more than one house during their lifetimes—generally, each one more expensive than the last—and often each comes with a brand-new thirty-year mortgage (in the game called "The Lifetime of Debt," I think that's the equivalent of "Going back to square one").

- Refinancing a mortgage is often an attempt to consolidate overwhelming debt from other sources, but, on average, about half of all refinances result in a higher overall loan amount. One step forward, two steps back.

- By the age of sixty, the average American has five or more credit cards; the average balance for households with credit card debt is $10,638; and the average American—right now—has thirteen outstanding credit obligations. And I don't mean "outstanding" in a good sort of way.

I know what you're probably thinking: *But today, being in debt is just part of life.* That's a primary point of disconnect between the "average American," like in the Credit Loan.com piece, and most cheapskates. With the possible exception of taking on a home mortgage, we simply don't believe that it's necessary to borrow money—or at least borrow so gosh darn much of it—to lead a happy, comfortable, even joyful life. Of the cheapskates I surveyed, at the time, more than 90 percent of them had no personal debt whatsoever, with the possible exception of a home mortgage.

Cheapskates understand the difference between "affordability" and what I call "borrowability." In other words, just because someone is willing to loan you the money to buy something, that doesn't mean you can afford it. Often, nothing could be further from the truth, as so many Americans sadly discovered during the collapse of the housing market.

We'll see real-life examples in the pages ahead about ways that cheapskates manage to keep debt out of their lives, and—when they do take on debt—how they've worked to pay it off as quickly as possible. But, in a nutshell, cheapskates still live by the old-school mantra: *If you can't afford to pay for it now, you simply can't afford it.*

"If I need to replace my car," one of my Miser Advisers once told me, "and all I have is $700 to spend, then I can tell you one thing: I'm going shopping for a $700 used car, *not* a new car where the $700 is just a down payment on a five-year car loan."

☞ *You might need a Cheapskate Intervention if you think a mortgage burning party is a possible alternative to foreclosure and involves hiring an arsonist.*

When it comes to the issue of retirement planning and debt, the cheapskates I've consulted have a particularly hard-assed position: as long as you have personal debt of any kind, *including a home mortgage*, you are not in a position to retire the cheapskate way. It's just that simple.

They feel so strongly about retiring debt-free, cheap-skates advise postponing retirement until you're able to pay off all outstanding debt, or even selling off other assets to eliminate debt. Another strategy is to downsize your life-style well before you retire (see Chapter 6), perhaps selling a house with an outstanding mortgage balance and using the proceeds of the sale to buy a less expensive home you can afford free and clear.

"The idea that most Americans retire while still owing on a home mortgage seems crazy to me," Rob Cartwright, one of my Miser Advisers from Arizona told me. "We just told ourselves that we would never do that," speaking of the retirement plans he and his wife Jenny had made. The Cartwrights ended up retiring their home mortgage—so they themselves could retire—by selling off approximately $60,000 in items they really didn't want to part with (including Rob's vintage motorcycle and some of Jenny's jewelry, among other valuables) but felt they must. "It was a tough decision," Rob admits, "but in the end we decided the value of spending time together, retiring sooner rather than later, was worth the tradeoff. So we stuck to our guns and had a mortgage burning party on the same day I retired."

Cheapskate Retirement Principle #2

One of the biggest assets you can have in retirement isn't something you have, but something you don't have—DEBT. Until you are entirely debt-free, including your home mortgage, you are not ready to retire the cheapskate way. Postpone retirement, sell off assets, or downsize your life/home, but do not retire until you are 100 percent debt-free.

IT'S THE THOUGHT—NOT THE SIZE— THAT MATTERS MOST

In the next chapter we're going to look more closely at the issue of retirement savings and how big of a nest egg you need to retire on.

But first, here's some happy, hopeful news for those who might end up retiring with a smaller egg than they'd like. According to another study by SunAmerica, when it comes to being happy and satisfied in retirement, the amount of time you spend planning and preparing for it in advance is actually more important than the absolute size of your retirement savings. The simple investment of your time in proactively planning for and envisioning your retirement is, when it comes to enjoying retirement, truly priceless.

The SunAmerica study states: "While it would appear that money is the key to satisfaction, the research found that there is a stronger correlation between satisfaction and length of time saving and preparing for retirement—regardless of net worth." That's all the more reason to get started planning for and thinking about your retirement today, particularly since those exercises are free, free, free!

THE CEDOTAL FAMILY

The Whole Wide World in Their Hands

I've always loved southern accents, and Shelle and Jonathan Cedotal could have been voice coaches for Scarlett O'Hara and Rhett Butler in *Gone with the Wind*. The couple live with their two boys, ages six and nine, in Jackson, Mississippi, a place Jonathan describes as "a big little town . . . just a bunch of little old country towns strung all together."

Both still in their mid-thirties, the Cedotals aren't planning on retiring anytime soon. In fact, neither Shelle nor Jonathan is certain they ever really want to fully retire. Shelle enjoys her part-time work as a registered nurse, and to hear Jonathan's enthusiasm when he talks about the small printing supply company he started in 2003 and still operates today, it's pretty clear that he's already among the "selfishly employed" (see Chapter 8).

"It's a quality-of-life kind of deal," Jonathan says, talking about being his own boss. "With your own business, you're not just earning an income, you're building an asset. Sure, you work hard, but you have your freedom. Sometimes I'm there on the weekends, and other days I just stop by to check in and then go on about my rat killing."

Sensing that "going on about one's rat killing" may be one of those sayings that loses something in translation when it crosses over the Mason-Dixon Line, Jonathan patiently backs up and explains to this clueless Yankee that it simply means "having the freedom to do as you please." I'm relieved to know that recreational rodent control isn't actually among this bright young businessman's hobbies.

What's compelling about the Cedotals' story—and why I wanted to interview them—is where they are in their financial lives compared with many similar families, and how they got there. While traditional, full-time retirement may or may not be something they'll ever decide they want in life, the important thing is that the young couple are already well on their way to achieving a level of financial independence that will give them the flexibility to choose as they please in the years ahead. Today, the couple live entirely debt-free, with the exception of their home mortgage, which they have been paying down at a breakneck pace and plan to have fully paid off before either hits age forty.

At this point in life, the Cedotals are fortunate to have a healthy income by national standards, and even more so by Mississippi standards, which in recent years has had the lowest median household income of any state in the union, according to the US Census Bureau. Last year, between the two of them, the Cedotals earned nearly $80,000, more than double the amount of the average Mississippi household. However, their income wasn't always that high, particularly as Jonathan was getting his business off the ground, and they say their income has grown by about $10,000 per year for each of the past five or six years.

The Cedotals were married young, very young, while he was still a seventeen-year-old senior in high school and Shelle had just turned eighteen and graduated. "We were high school sweethearts, and I was afraid Shelle would go off to college and find somebody better, so I figured we should get married. Best thing I've done yet," Jonathan says with a big smile.

Later in the interview, Jonathan makes what strikes me as a truly profound observation: he attributes a goodly part of the couple's current financial success to the fact that they *did* marry very young—although they also held off eight years before having their first child—and, unlike nearly half of all couples who get married today, they've stayed married. "I know a guy my age who's just now getting married for the first time," Jonathan says. "They're planning a $20,000 wedding, honeymoon in Jamaica, the whole nine yards," adding that when he and Shelle married, they just put a notice in the local paper and spent their honeymoon in a nearby hotel. "So now he's just starting off, planning to have kids and all, while Shelle and I are through all of that and even thinking about retirement and stuff like that. A lot of times, I think the earlier in life you do some things, the better."

But like many young newlyweds, the money was going out significantly faster than it was coming in when the Cedotals were first married. Jonathan was working at a grocery store and later at Walmart, and Shelle was taking classes in nursing at Northeast Louisiana University and holding down a part-time job at Roto-Rooter. "We had almost a negative income at that time. . . . I don't know if it could have gone any lower," Shelle says.

The young couple managed to buy a used mobile home for $6,000, which they lived in and later sold for $11,000, and then upgraded to a new-used mobile home costing $11,000, which they sold after Hurricane Katrina for $17,000. "The secret to finding out what used stuff is really worth and whether you'll get your money out of it when you go to sell it is to check what it's actually selling for on Craigslist, not some Blue Book," Jonathan says. He refers to Craigslist as "a way of life for buyers and sellers" like himself, claiming to have bought and sold more than $70,000 worth of items on Craigslist over the years. Most of his transactions have netted the couple a tidy profit. The Cedotals' success in flipping their used mobile homes for a profit—something many financial pundits consider a fool's errand—is proof of their cheapskate business savvy.

But by the time Jonathan decided he wanted to take the plunge and attempt to start a business of his own (technically, a franchise), the couple had managed to rack up some pretty significant debt, despite their modest living conditions. "We had two car loans, $27,000 in student loans from my time in school, and about $5,000 in credit card debt," Shelle recalls.

As Jonathan was getting his new business started, the couple was living off Shelle's nursing income alone, taking home less than $600 per week. Jonathan admits that things were dicey for the couple at that point, with his not being able to pay himself a salary out of his still fragile new company, and admitting that the business was being cash-flowed mostly on credit cards. With about $50,000 of debt hanging over their heads, a new business venture with a very uncertain future, and their first son being born earlier that year, by late 2003 the Cedotals were spending some pretty sleepless nights.

I'm always fascinated when I meet folks like the Cedotals—people who have managed to relatively quickly pay off significant amounts of debt—and to hear about their "triggers." What is it that prompts some people to take control of their finances, rather than continue to let their finances control them, as so many others do? Over the years, I've heard a lot of stories about different "triggers" that have motivated people to get on top of their debts and other financial woes, everything from psychiatry and debt and marriage counseling to religious epiphanies, family emergencies, and even near-death experiences (seriously).

But the wake-up call that motivated the Cedotals to get their financial house in order is one I'd never heard before. "It was a Caribbean cruise," according to Shelle. When Jonathan started his business, the franchise company sent a few of the new franchisees and their spouses on a free five-day cruise to Mexico. "Neither of us had ever traveled outside the United States before . . . heck, the most we'd ever traveled in our whole lives was no more than four or five hours from home. And, you know, a light just came on," she says. "It made us realize that there's a whole wide world out there, and even though we live in a small town in Mississippi where most people don't do this sort of thing (world travel), we could actually go out there and see it . . . but only if we didn't have debt and if we set our priorities on what we really wanted—the big things in life—instead of wasting money on the small stuff."

Upon returning from that life-changing cruise, the Cedotals were hyperenergized about getting out of debt— for good—and whipping their finances into shape. Jonathan is quick to credit Shelle for being the real driving force behind getting the family's financial ship turned around, inspiring him to be more fiscally responsible as part of the process. "Our approach was kind of like burning the boats," Jonathan says, using another expression that left me visibly clueless. "You know, like with invading armies in the old days? They'd burn their boats after they landed so there was no way to retreat. They were in it to win or else." Jonathan is a true polite southern gentleman, but I can see he's thinking to himself, *Don't these northerners know anything?*

"We started throwing everything extra we had at our debts and stopped taking on new ones," Shelle says. They literally cut up each of their credit cards as they paid them off. The Cedotals are big fans of the Christian-oriented personal finance expert Dave Ramsey. They used the "snowballing" approach he prescribes for paying down debt, which, rather uniquely, encourages people to pay off their smallest debts first (not necessarily those with the highest interest rates) as a way of building and maintaining enthusiasm for seeing the process through until the end. Kind of like burning your boats—or credit cards—I suppose.

Within about two and a half years, the Cedotals had retired all of their personal debt, with the exception of the mortgage on the handsome new brick home they had subcontracted themselves—a $181,000 investment (including the land) that was valued at $270,000+, even after the housing market collapse. With their other debt off their backs, they then began aggressively paying down their mortgage, many months paying two or even three times the required amount. At the current pace, it will have taken them only eleven years to pay off their home in full.

But that's not the end of the Cedotals' boat burning, or is that rat killing? They've also managed to create an emergency fund with six months' worth of living expenses in it (including money for mortgage payments), fund Roth IRAs for their retirement, and set aside $100 each month in a "Play Money Account." "I get our weekly allotment of 'play money' out of the ATM in cash every Monday, like clockwork, but we find that we have a hard time even spending it, because there's so many things to do that don't cost a penny," Shelle says.

When it comes to raising their sons, Wesley and Will, it's clear that the Cedotals are loving, caring parents. Right down to the point where—and I mean this sincerely, and have witnessed it in many other parents I call "cheapskates" in the most positive sense of the term—one of their primary concerns is *not* giving their children everything they want as soon as they want it. You might say parents like the Cedotals love their kids too much to spoil them. Shelle tells the story of one of her sons being teased by another boy about not having a pair of the latest designer tennis shoes. "I told him, 'You just tell your little friend that next time he sees our family taking off on a cruise ship to see the world, *that's* what we spend our money on instead.'"

Here's another example of creative cheapskate parenting, where the focus is on "fun" and not "funds." Last Christmas, Shelle had the brilliant idea of surprising the boys with what they both say is one of their favorite gifts of all times: a dump truck full of topsoil costing $120, delivered. "Seriously. Have you ever seen boys play in a huge mound of dirt? Do you know how many toy cars and army men have spent the night on that mound of dirt?" Shelle says. "They also got about $40 worth of toys from Santa, but the pile was the star attraction for them that Christmas." Jonathan adds that they specifically had the dirt dumped in a low spot in the yard, "So once . . . *if* . . . the boys ever lose interest, it won't go to waste (wink)." Try doing that with a $400 Xbox.

As Jonathan's business has grown and continues to thrive, he and Shelle have thought a lot about what they want to *give* their children, as opposed to insisting that their sons *earn* things on their own just as Jonathan and Shelle have their whole lives. The Cedotals would like to see their sons go to college—if that's what their sons decide they want—but they say it's likely to involve the boys starting out at a local community college and helping to earn their own way through a four-year degree program, again in the tradition of *life lessons* being at least as important as *classroom lessons* in the eyes of Shelle and Jonathan.

As for Shelle and Jonathan themselves, with their current finances shipshape and their future looking even brighter, they're in no hurry—and certainly no panic—about deciding what their retirement will look like. "I just think life is going to get a lot easier after forty," Jonathan says, referring mostly to when their house is paid off and his business is fully established.

At this point, Jonathan is thinking they'll hang on to ownership of his business, but maybe hire someone to manage it as he gets older. He and Shelle talk about the possibility of doing some missionary work through their church and, of course, being able to travel. "I think if we want to just get up and go, we'll have the freedom to do it," he says. Or, as I've grown fond of saying since first meeting him, "go on about their rat killing."

CHAPTER 3

How Much Money Do You Really *Need to Retire?*

I'm skeptical, to say the least, when it comes to rules of thumb and other one-size-fits-all formulas often applied in financial planning. But based on my personal experience— and supported by countless other cheapskates I've spoken with—I have developed a pair of financial aphorisms of my own that I believe to be irrefutably true:

The Big Binder Theorem: "There exists a direct correlation between how much you pay for a financial planning service—or how much you will **eventually** pay if you purchase the financial products recommended by the service—and how elaborate the binder notebook is containing those recommendations."

The Big Binder Corollary Theorem: "There generally exists an inverse relationship between how elaborate a financial planning binder is and the usefulness and practicality of the information it contains."

Okay, maybe I'm being a bit too cynical, but I think a lot of people can relate. My advice is just to be on your guard whenever you're given a financial planning binder that:

- Has more than three rings.
- Is over 1.5 inches thick.
- Has color-coded tabs, tabs using Roman numerals, and/or more than eight tabs of any kind.
- Includes a plastic sleeve or pouch, regardless of what's inside of it.
- Uses any type of paper clip or other fastening device you've never seen before.
- Contains a combination of ten or more of any of the following (aka "the Chinese Menu Test"): color pie charts or graphs, PowerPoint slides with your name on them, business cards of firm members, or references to you by name in the body of the text. (Add three points for any references intended to refer to you, but through a word processing glitch instead refer to a previous recipient of the Big Binder. For example, "This customized financial plan was prepared specifically for Mr. Guy Gullible," when your name is Mr. Tony Tightwad.)

Become Your Own CFO ("Chief Frugal Officer")

No matter how "customized" (as evidenced by how often your name appears in the body of the text), most retirement and other expertly prepared financial plans are ultimately retreads of a handful of one-size-fits-all financial planning models that populate finance-related websites like popup ads for Viagra on a porn site. In all seriousness, cheapskates are frequently skeptical of personalized financial plans, formulas, and other advice proffered by most financial planners. In my 2009 survey of self-described cheapskates, I found that only about one in ten cheapskates consulted a financial planner on a regular basis, and fewer than half had *ever* used one.

And there are at least two good reasons for that healthy skepticism among cheapskates when it comes to professional financial planners and the advice they offer. First, that advice nearly always comes at a cost, and one that is often much higher than might seem apparent. Financial planners can charge for their services in a number of different ways, including:

- **Commissions on "investment products" they sell you:** For example, front-end sales loads on mutual funds or commissions paid directly to the planner for the sale of insurance products.
- **A percentage of your account value:** Usually ranging from 0.50 to 2.5 percent annually. Sometimes planners collect both commissions and a percentage of account value, which is, confusingly, termed a "fee-based" structure (as opposed to a "fee-only" adviser).
- **An hourly rate, flat fee, or annual retainer:** These are billing approaches typically used by "fee-only" plan-

ners, although the fee may be charged as a percentage of the assets they manage for you. The primary difference is that fee-only advisers can receive compensation only from you, thereby reducing any incentive on the part of the adviser to sell you investment products simply to collect commissions. In general, as you might guess, when cheapskates are in the market for financial advice, we prefer fee-only advisers. (To find fee-only advisers in your area, consult the website of the National Association of Personal Financial Advisers: www.napfa.org.)

Even more important, most professionally generated retirement plans are based on formulas and other suppositions that simply don't apply to cheapskates, because they fail to fully take into account how different the spending side of the equation is for us frugal folks. Instead, they start from the premise that an individual's cost of living (in retirement as well as before retirement) is a factor of his or her income. So in calculating "your number"—the size of the nest egg the experts say you'll need to have in order to retire—they often gloss over the fact that cheapskates don't spend and live like typical Americans before they retire, and they have no intention of beginning to do so once they retire.

In fairness to financial planners, their income-based formulas for retirement planning may in fact make sense for "typical Americans." After all, with so many people failing to prove their ability to live below or even within their means prior to retirement, why should a planner assume that they will successfully trim their spending after they retire? For example, a 2012 study by Bankrate.com found that 46 percent of Americans have more in outstanding credit card debt than they have in savings set aside for an emergency. I say that that situation in and of itself constitutes an emergency!

On top of that type of sketchy fiscal track record, planners don't want to take the risk of advising people to save too little for retirement, so their clients might run out of money before they run out of time. And, of course, all those planners who work on commission want to sell clients just as many investment products as possible, which always seems like a potential conflict of interest to me.

Because of all of this, cheapskates know that we must become our own top financial advisers. It's too important a job to trust to someone else or to rely on formulas that rarely apply to us, the way we live, and—most of all—the way we spend and view money so differently. Sure, seek any outside professional help you may need, including fee-only financial advisers, tax professionals, legal counsel, and so on, but you need to be the world's leading expert on your own finances and retirement plans. You need to be the CFO (Chief Frugal Officer) of your own life.

Particularly when it comes to knowing and controlling (or deciding not to control) the spending side of your personal finances, no one—no matter what their education or professional background—can be more of an expert than you.

Cheapskates know that there's no passing the buck, literally or figuratively, when it comes to offloading onto others the ultimate responsibility for managing your own finances and planning for your own retirement.

Cheapskate Retirement Principle #3

Use the services of professional financial planners cautiously, understanding in advance the costs associated with those services (including any hidden agendas in terms of selling you commission-based investment products) and the fact that many planners refuse to believe that cheapskates can live so well on so little. Even if you consult a planner, use his or her services simply as a second opinion, a reality check on the financial plans you have developed. Remember, you— and only you—are the Chief Frugal Officer when it comes to your retirement planning.

The Myth of the Million-Dollar Mantra

When most people start thinking about and planning for retirement, they're likely to stumble across a few pearls of wisdom from financial planners and the investment industry, the upshot of which is that many people then promptly *stop* thinking about and planning for retirement. Why bother? When you do the math and plug your own numbers into these equations for determining how much the experts say you'll need to amass in savings before you can comfortably retire, suddenly the national debt doesn't look so daunting after all.

That's a real shame, because we all know that the sooner you start to save for retirement, the easier it is to build your nest egg. Too often these retirement planning formulas have the effect of paralyzing people, particularly younger people, who simply decide the mountain ahead of them is too high, so why even bother to start climbing?

But one piece of advice most financial planners will share that *is* true is that when it comes to investing for retirement, the "time horizon" is critical. By being demoralized to the point of not starting to put away *any* money for retirement from the very start of your working years—even if it's just a few dollars a week—young people are throwing away one of the greatest assets they have: time, time for small savings to grow into big savings.

☞ *You might need a Cheapskate Intervention if you confuse "annuitizing" with "martinizing" whenever you go to either a financial adviser or a dry cleaner. (By the way, both are likely to leave you hung out to dry.)*

If you're just starting to think about retirement and have yet to encounter these retirement planning formulas designed to shock and awe, they typically state that you will need at least 80 to 90 percent of your preretirement income in order to live comfortably in retirement. Some financial pundits go even further, suggesting that to really play it safe, you should have in place a retirement plan capable of generating 100 percent—or even 110 percent!—of your pre-retirement income.

Once they've broken that news to you (usually under tab 2 in the Big Binder, often accompanied by a cartoon-ish figure of a stressed-out retiree who has just realized he's saved too little), then it's pretty straightforward math to figure out how large a retirement nest egg you'll need. After adding together any income you can expect from what are sometimes called "guaranteed sources" (including Social Security and any employer-provided pensions or income from annuities), the difference between that total and the aforementioned 80 to 110 percent of your preretirement in-come needs to come from so-called "variable sources."

Variable sources include any retirement investments (e.g., a 401(k) or IRA) and other savings of your own, as well as the possibility of liquidating or otherwise tapping any fixed assets (like the equity in your home) for additional income during retirement. And if you plan on continuing to work at least part-time during retirement, that projected income is also considered "variable," since you can't entirely control it (e.g., a health problem prevents you from working, or you simply can't find a job).

Of course, the experts also say you need to be very care-ful when it comes to tapping your nest egg (i.e., your "variable sources") to make up that difference between income from your "guaranteed sources" and the 80 to 110 percent of your preretirement income that they claim you'll need to live on in retirement. Most financial planners suggest that you plan to draw no more than 3 or 4 percent annually from your own savings in order to keep ahead of inflation and avoid depleting your nest egg before you die.

Sure, everybody's situation is different. But if you play around with these basic formulas a little bit, you're likely to have the devastating epiphany that every financial planner I've ever met seems to be secretly, longingly waiting to watch you discover: "Oh my God! I need a million dollars— and probably even more—before I can retire!" Ah yes, *the Million-Dollar Mantra.*

After all, using these standard retirement planning rules of thumb, it's not hard to come to that conclusion. This is a simple example, but let's say you have a preretirement income of $60,000 and—since you're determined to become more of a cheapskate after you retire—you believe you can live on only 85 percent of that amount in retirement. That means you'll need an annual income of $51,000 in your first year of retirement, with cost-of-living increases factored in going forward.

Like nearly three-quarters of all Americans today, you're not lucky enough to have a traditional pension provided by your employer(s), one that would guarantee you an income stream for life. Nor do you have any annuities to provide additional fixed income. So the only income other than what you draw from your 401(k) and other savings will be Social

Security, which, based on your work history, you calculate will be about $1,700 per month, or $20,400 per year.

That leaves a difference of $30,600 per year to be made up from your nest egg. Assuming you withdraw 3 percent annually from your nest egg, that means—you guessed it— you need roughly ONE MILLION DOLLARS ($1,020,000, to be exact) in retirement savings in order to generate the level of income the experts insist you'll need to live on in retirement. And if the outcome of that simple story problem doesn't sufficiently knock the breath out of you, the financial planner is inevitably all too eager to add: "Remember, that million-dollar figure doesn't include the value of your home, either!"

I've often thought that some really savvy financial planner would come up with the idea of including an airsickness bag in the front flap of the Big Binder to keep the client from embarrassing himself when he comes to the part about how much you'll need to save for retirement.

Don't Say "Variable Annuities," or I'll Bark like a Dog

In my own life, I first butted heads with the Million-Dollar Mantra when I was still midstream in my career in the non-profit sector, before I quit the workaday world to become selfishly employed as a writer.

At the urging of a friend, I reluctantly agreed to meet

with a financial planner he knew to discuss our retirement plans. The planner was a nice enough guy, and I even gave him the benefit of the doubt when I saw that he had a photo of himself on his business card—something that normally triggers from me a stream of sarcastic comments.

At that time, both my wife and I were working full-time in jobs that paid relatively well for our chosen professions, and our combined annual income was nearly $75,000. We were living comfortably, although we've never lived excessively. In fact—as I took great care to explain to the planner at our initial meeting—we were spending only about half of what we earned, including the payments we were still making on our home mortgage.

As I told the planner, our secret for living on such a small portion of our income was that my wife and I had made a pact early in our marriage to establish what we called a "permanent standard of living." We had decided a few years after we married that we were quite content and happy living at the level we were then enjoying, so we made a conscious decision to avoid the common trap of allowing one's lifestyle (and spending) to escalate as one's earnings increase. It meant that initially we were simply living within our means, but with each passing year—as our salaries grew—we were increasingly living below our means, and all without a sense of sacrifice or deprivation. Of course, our actual dollar-amount spending to maintain our "permanent standard of living" was occasionally adjusted for inflation, but in reality it grew very little over the years.

That lifestyle included living in a comfortable but afford-able house that we were remodeling ourselves as our bud-get allowed and that we planned to live in for a good many years, maybe even forever. We had two ancient but road-worthy vehicles, and placed no value whatsoever on driving a fancy car; we generally bought used vehicles and drove them until they dropped. We enjoyed spending simple time together, pursuing a number of inexpensive pastimes, some of which—like cooking, gardening, and home remodeling—actually saved us a lot of money to boot. One of our greatest passions was world travel, something we pinched our pen-nies all the more in order to be able to afford, although we were happiest traveling "cheapskate-style," avoiding package tours and luxury travel, and preferring travel that allowed us to live like and get to know the people in the places we visited.

For a variety of personal reasons, we had decided early in our marriage to not have or adopt children, a decision that now nearly one in five American couples makes. That decision was not based on economics, although obviously the cost of raising children is significant. Had we had chil-dren, clearly we would have had to have established a dif-ferent "permanent standard of living," one that allowed for their care, education, and so on. But as we'll see throughout this book, "cheapskates with kids" typically adopt this same basic approach for living below their means, proving that it is indeed possible even in families with children.

So when I met with the financial planner that day, I

explained all of this in excruciating detail. I emphasized over and over again that while we were currently earning almost $75,000, we were spending only about half of that. I also discussed the fact that when our home mortgage was fully paid off (something we were on the fast track to do early, well before we retired), we'd be able to live on even less, with no monthly mortgage payment to make. I discussed with the planner that in retirement we might decide to indulge our passion for world travel even more—keeping it cheapskate-style, of course—but that increased spending would easily be more than offset by what we were no longer spending on mortgage payments. Suffice it to say, I thought I had explained the spending side of our lives pretty clearly and thoroughly.

I noticed that the planner's eyes glazed over early on in the conversation, and more than once I caught a glimpse of him staring listlessly at the picture of himself on his business card, which still lay on the desk between us. He also didn't take a single note during our meeting, which rather surprised me, but I figured he might have a photographic memory, since he had a photographic business card. Finally, he snapped out of his apparent coma, like a daft audience member who's been recruited up on stage by a hypnotist in a Las Vegas show and then told to return to his seat and bark like a dog whenever anybody says the words "variable annuities."

The planner then handed me a three-page checklist of tax and other financial documents I would need to assemble and send to him in order for his firm to develop our "custom-ized retirement plan." I left his office feeling anxious and a little frustrated, so much so that I forgot to pick up his busi-ness card-cum-senior-class-photo from the desk.

☞ *You might need a Cheapskate Intervention if your retirement portfolio consists of an envelope full of scratch-off tickets.*

Nonetheless, the following week I assembled the re-quested documents and sent them off to the planner. Later that month, he informed me that our plan was ready and that he thought I'd be "awesomely excited" with what he'd come up with.

With hope anew (I rarely get "awesomely excited"), I at-tended the scheduled follow-up meeting at his office. I was seated by his secretary at a massive conference table con-taining an even more massive notebook with the names of my wife and me embossed on the cover. As I leafed through it superficially, it appeared as if most of the material in the binder consisted simply of photocopies of the reams of per-sonal documents I had originally provided to the planner. I can't remember for sure, but I think I barked once at that point.

By the time the financial planner entered the room, I had already lost all patience with the exercise and asked him to skip the preliminaries—including the color charts, bar graphs, and all the material I had provided to him so that he could simply photocopy it, punch holes in it, and hand it back to me.

"Listen," I said as politely as I could, "unfortunately I'm short on time. What I'm most interested in is how much income you think we'll need to live on in retirement and how big of a nest egg we'll need in order to generate that income."

"Oh, Jeff," he said, sliding another one of his photogenic business cards to me across the table like a blackjack dealer in a Brooks Brothers suit. "I thought we covered that in the first meeting. You'll need *at least* 85 to 90 percent—and probably more—of your preretirement income to live on in retirement. That's the rule. There's nothing anybody can do about that."

I put my head down on top of the Big Binder on the conference table and again began to bark out loud. At least I think I did.

"Um," he continued, a little taken aback by my demeanor, "you'll see under Tab 13 that we've projected that you'll need retirement savings of about $1 million . . . actually, I think it was $1.2 million or something like that . . . just to be safe. And since by the time you retire, your income will have likely grown, you'll need even more to generate 85 to 90 percent of that larger income. Kind of like a chicken-and-egg thing, if you follow me."

What I wanted to say was, "I not only follow you, but I've already lapped you a couple of times." Instead, I thanked him for his time, and told him a bald-faced lie. "Gee," I said. "There's so much in this notebook to review, I'll look it over and get back to you," and I left his office lugging the Big Binder under my arm.

To this day, the "Confidential Retirement Plan—Developed Expressly for Denise & Jeffrey Yeager" occupies the same position and serves the same vital purpose as the day I brought it home: a perfect water-absorbing plant stand for under the potted money tree in my office.

Cheapskate Retirement Principle #4

Retirement planning formulas that use your preretirement income as the basis for projecting your retirement income needs—and the assets necessary to generate that income—are highly inaccurate for most cheapskates, since they rarely live on 100 percent of their income before retirement. Instead, to retire the cheapskate way, you must crunch the actual expense numbers yourself and then determine the size of the nest egg you need to hatch.

Getting Real: Reality Retirement Planning

So, the bad news is that as your own Chief Frugal Officer, the responsibility falls solely on you to really crunch your own numbers and figure out that most important element of retirement planning: how much will you *actually* need to live on in retirement, given your lifestyle and retirement dreams and expectations? It's very likely that that exercise will prompt you to rethink some of the ways you spend money today, and how you plan to spend money and live in retirement. And that's usually a good thing.

To begin to get a handle on how much you'll spend in retirement—and therefore how much you'll actually need to amass in savings before you retire—there are two main issues to consider: (1) How much are you spending currently, before retirement? (2) Will your spending change—either decrease or perhaps increase—once you are retired?

I won't lie to you (call me cheap, but never call me a liar). Answering these two questions is going to take some serious thinking, calculating, reflecting, modifying, and even soul searching. The goal isn't to be conservative in your spending projections or to lowball your projections; the goal is to be as accurate as humanly possible in your projections. And that's going to take some time and hard work on your part. No one can do it for you, even if he does have a photo of himself on his business cards.

Like most Americans, you might not know how or even how much money you're currently spending. Don't feel bad; only about 10 percent of American households have a formal budget and track their spending against it. Figuring that out is the first step. The second step—if you're an aspiring cheapskate—is to try to reduce that spending as much as possible, immediately, even before retirement. Then, and only then, the final step is to look into your crystal ball and put some actual numbers next to the items you foresee spending money on in retirement.

The good news is that to help you find your way through that rigorous exercise—and learn some new things and even have a little fun along the way—I've developed "The Ultimate Cheapskate's Bodacious Retirement Budgetary Worksheet," located on my website, www.UltimateCheapskate.com.

As you'll see, my Bodacious Retirement Budgetary Worksheet not only allows you to plot your current spending, your goals for reducing spending, and your estimated spending once you retire, it also gives you information on the average amounts other people spend on various items once they've retired, as a frame of reference. Best of all, the worksheet is annotated with Internet and other resources so you can learn more about how to reduce your spending on various expense items. And—if you dig around enough—you'll even uncover some special surprises I've hidden in there to amuse and amaze you. If only the Internal Revenue Service let me design their forms for them.

But before you rush off to start exploring my Bodacious Retirement Budgetary Worksheet, here's some other potentially good news you should think about, even for folks not consciously planning to scale back on their spending in retirement: Some research suggests that most people voluntarily— perhaps even unwittingly—spend less as they age.

In a 2005 article entitled "Reality Retirement Planning:

A New Paradigm for an Old Science," published in the *Journal of Financial Planning*, financial planner Ty Bernicke argues that spending appears to voluntarily decrease with age, something that he has observed firsthand with many of his clients and which is supported by data from the US Bureau of Labor Statistics' Consumer Expenditure Survey. In every major expense category of the survey other than health care, people appear to naturally spend progressively less as they age (at least from their peak career years forward), despite the fact that their household wealth continues to grow as they age, suggesting that they could in fact afford to spend more—not less—if they so chose.

Bernicke writes: "Traditional retirement planning assumes that a household's expenditures will increase a certain amount each year throughout retirement. Yet data from the US Bureau of Labor's Consumer Expenditure Survey show that household expenditures actually decline as retirees age. Consequently, under traditional retirement planning, consumers tend to oversave for retirement, underspend in their early years of retirement, or postpone retirement."

Jean Setzfand, vice president of financial security at the American Association of Retired Persons (AARP), told me in an interview that her experience with AARP members and some of the organization's internal research supports the idea that many people tend to spend less, not more, as they age and settle into retirement. She believes that the reasons for that phenomenon are varied but noted that some of the organization's "ethnographic research" suggests something that seems rather counterintuitive. "People who haven't thought about what their retirement is going to look like—those who don't have a proactive plan—oftentimes become sort of financially paralyzed once they're retired and have a hard time deciding how to spend their money."

Setzfand describes that variety of retirees as having a "pension mentality," people whose work provided most of the structure in their lives, and without it they're rudder-less when it comes to how to spend their time . . . and their money. "If you're proactive in planning for retirement and you can envision what it's going to be like, the money plan will follow," she says. I have another déjà vu moment, think-ing back to my conversation thirty years ago with my friend Bob Johnson and his comment about "the money stuff really isn't that hard."

Regardless of causes, as you can see from the table on page 68, even after factoring in increased health-care costs, annual consumer spending drops by 45 percent between its peak in the forty-five- to fifty-four-year age bracket and the seventy-five-year-plus bracket, something that seems lost in most financial planning. While many retirement plan-ning models allow for some projected decrease in spending at the point of retirement for job-related expenses you'll no longer have (e.g., commuting costs, professional wardrobe ex-penses, lunches out, etc.), most assume that after that initial adjustment your expenses will climb each year by 3 percent or more, simply based on projected increases in consumer prices.

ANNUAL CONSUMER SPENDING BY AGE

Spending category	Under 25 years	25–34 years	35–44 years	45–54 years	55–64 years	65–74 years	75+ years
Apparel and services	1,559	2,087	2,040	1,966	1,571	1,186	708
Entertainment	1,221	2,251	3,058	3,088	2,683	2,341	1,374
Food and alcohol	4,479	6,564	7,980	7,644	6,470	5,540	4,057
Healthcare[1]	775	1,800	2,583	3,261	3,859	4,922	4,754
Housing[2]	9,553	16,845	20,041	18,900	16,673	14,420	11,421
Transportation	4,692	8,231	8,763	9,255	8,111	6,086	4,288
Personal insurance and pensions[3]	2,036	5,318	6,944	7,668	6,403	2,648	996
Miscellaneous[4]	3,166	3,521	4,537	6,005	5,131	4,293	3,931
TOTALS	27,481	46,617	55,946	57,787	50,901	41,436	31,529

Source: U.S. Department of Labor, Bureau of Labor Statistics, Consumer Expenditure Survey, 2010
[1] Includes both health insurance premiums as well as out-of-pocket costs for medical services, drugs, and supplies. [2] Includes mortgage and rental costs, as well as property taxes, utilities, maintenance/repairs, furnishings, appliances, and other household services and supplies. [3] Includes life and other personal insurances, as well as payments into pensions and Social Security. [4] Includes personal care products and services, reading material, education, tobacco products, cash contributions, and other miscellaneous expenses.

What Bernicke calls "reality retirement planning" (as opposed to "traditional retirement planning") anticipates the likely, ongoing decrease in spending reflected in the US Bureau of Labor Statistics' survey throughout retirement—although, like traditional retirement planning, the reality model also anticipates increased spending due to inflation. "Reality retirement planning is like a tug-of-war match, with inflation pulling spending needs up and human nature's tendencies pulling spending back down," Bernicke writes. "Ultimately, this tug of war more accurately depicts the average American's spending patterns throughout retirement."

By Bernicke's use of the phrase "tug-of-war," one might imagine that the tendency to naturally spend less as we age (as reflected in the USBLS survey) is pretty much a wash with a projected annual inflation rate of 3 or 4 percent. In other words, you might expect that in the end, the tug-of-war ends in a tie.

☞ *You might need a Cheapskate Intervention if your idea of asset allocation is to bet on the same horse to win, place, and show.*

But when you apply the suppositions behind reality retirement planning to some hypothetical situations, the outcome is anything but a Mexican standoff. In his article, Bernicke uses the example of a couple with an $800,000 retirement nest egg and a need for $60,000 in after-tax spending money in their first year of retirement, which they hope will be at age fifty-five.

Using a traditional retirement planning model that assumes that the couple's expenses will increase each year by 3 percent due to inflation, their spending needs will increase to more than $145,000 per year by the time they reach age eighty-five. The problem is, even if their nest egg earns an average of 8 percent annually and both spouses start drawing Social Security at age sixty-two, their ever-increasing withdrawals would likely deplete their savings by age eighty-one. Under this traditional retirement planning model, the couple would either need to delay retirement by about seven years or decrease their spending by about 20 percent annually in order to avoid running out of money.

However, with the reality retirement planning approach, when you project that the same couple's spending will naturally decrease in the same proportions reflected in the USBLS survey, by the age of eighty-five, the couple's nest egg would have *grown* to a whopping $2,364,871 (less taxes paid on unused required minimum distributions from 401(k) withdrawals), rather than being long since depleted. This assumes the same rate of return on their investments and same inflation rate as in the above example.

Of course any hypothetical example is only that. In real life, emergencies can happen, and Bernicke also acknowledges that his research doesn't factor in long-term care expenses (although, in fairness, most traditional retirement planning doesn't specifically allocate money for such care either). But for those of us prepared and creative enough to really ratchet down spending even further when we retire, it's encouraging to know that the forces of human nature might be pushing us along that same path as well. Now, just think about how much further we can stretch our nest eggs if we really put our backs into it, cheapskate-style.

Cheapskate Retirement Principle #5

Don't underestimate your income needs during retirement, but do take into consideration the evidence that for most people—cheapskates as well as spendthrifts— their spending tends to naturally decline as they age during their retirement years. The important exception to this trend is health-care costs, which tend to increase with age.

Does Aging Really Cause "IF" ("Increased Frugality")?

When you stop and think about it, the premise behind "reality retirement planning"—that people's spending tends to naturally taper off as they age—is only common sense. As most people age, they and their lifestyles slow down, which means their spending generally slows down, too. You're likely to travel less, saving not just on leisure-travel costs, but also on daily wear and tear on your car and fuel costs. You'll probably pursue less active—and less costly—hobbies and other pastimes as you grow older. The survey data show that people also tend to spend less on entertainment as they age, and even eat and drink less.

It also stands to reason that by the time you reach your truly golden years, you're likely to have already acquired whatever toys and trinkets you coveted earlier in life . . . or have decided that at this point they're no longer worth acquiring. And if you're ever going to pay off your #$*@ home mortgage while you're still residing aboveground—or decide to move into a smaller, more affordable home—it's likely to be in your retirement years if it is to be at all.

In response to an article I wrote on this topic in January 2012 for my "Cheap Talk" blog on the AARP website (http://blog.aarp.org/author/jeffyeagerultimatecheapskate), there was strong agreement among most readers who commented on the question I asked: Are you becoming more frugal with age? Most respondents said yes, their non-health-care-related spending has definitely decreased—even dramatically so—with age. The interesting thing, though, was some of the reasons, stories, and explanations readers gave regarding this phenomenon:

"Yes, I am getting cheaper the older I get. I think I am getting ready to live on a fixed income." (Wendy L. Dietze, 60)

"I believe I have become more frugal with age, at least on some things. I bring my lunch to work and have my own coffeepot at work to brew my own instead of buying it anywhere. On the other hand, I have a daughter in a private kindergarten, a new car payment, and other bills that make me become more frugal on these sorts of things." (Bill Camp, 39)

"As a retired 63 year old female, I find spending my savings after a lifetime of frugality is really hard. I always delighted in seeing how far I could stretch my money and how much I could save; and now, I don't have to anymore. However, I still do, because I still love the challenge of getting value. I feel so guilty when I pay full price for anything. I've started traveling, something I didn't do before retirement. For some reason, I don't feel guilty spending on travel, maybe because I am getting value by all the knowledge I learn from my traveling experiences. I just love being retired—I couldn't have done it without being frugal." (Anonymous)

"Yes, because I want to do more with my money than ever before." (Cecilia Cumberland, 34)

"No! I figure I might as well spend it or someone else will!" (Lee Jacintho, 74)

"I am frugal in different ways than when I was a young woman, single mother, or older worker at the management level preparing for retirement. All those stages of my life required their own sets of priorities and required any income to be carefully managed. I lived by the creed 'Use it up, wear it out, make it do, do without.' Because of that, I can now live comfortably using common sense." (Anonymous)

"Being frugal is second nature when you're raised in a large family by parents who grew up during the Depression." (Mary Jackson Wooley, 70)

"I just turned 30 and I can definitely see how I have become more frugal from just 7–10 years ago. I would spend my whole paycheck in one weekend and not have any money for the next two weeks, and I was constantly overdrafting my checking account, having to pay fees. Never had any money saved, and didn't care about spending $12 on lunch or $3 for a cup of coffee, would play the lottery every week and blow an average of $50 a week with nothing to show for it. . . . I had to sit down and realize that I'm not going to DIE if I don't always spend money. It's actually quite liberating." (Anonymous)

"As we get older we also realize all the things we can do without!" (Karen Callinan, 60)

"I think that's true. I put a 10-year-old shirt in the rag bag, and my mom took it out and has been wearing it for at least another ten years." (Deborah Torres, 50)

"Part of it is that we remember when everything cost so much less. We have a hard time accepting today's prices, and so we just don't spend!" (Fred Smith, 73)

"I've grown more frugal over the years. Part of it springs from necessity (disability payments aren't much!), but another part is that I've learned that I really don't need many things in life in order to be happy and content." (Lisa Denny, 53)

"With every passing year, I'm starting to appreciate more and more that saying 'The best things in life aren't things.'" (Al Hanson, 47)

"Like a lot of activities when you get older, shopping becomes more a chore than something you really enjoy doing. At this point, even if there's something I still want that I don't already have—which isn't much, LOL!—I'm hesitant to go out and buy it because I don't want to leave my kids even more 'stuff' that they'll need to go sort through and figure out what to do with once I'm gone." (Florence Biles, 77)

"Of course. It costs a lot less to spoil my five grandkids than it did to raise my two children!" (Ellen Coyle, 66)

"Because both sets of our parents lived through the Depression as adults, we were each raised with a frugal mind-set. Even so, we have become more frugal with age. My husband took early retirement in late 2010, and we are aggressively paying down our mortgage with his retirement income so that the house payment will be gone by the time I retire." (Anonymous)

"Not that I've ever been into 'keeping up with the Joneses,' as they say, but by this point in my life I couldn't give a flying fig about social status and keeping up appearances. Life is too short for that, particularly at my age." (Fred Fields, 88)

"The other day the guys at work were razzing me because I don't have cable. But I'm the only one out of the whole crew that has no mortgage, car payment, or credit card debt. Being frugal gives peace of mind." (Jim Miller, 43)

"I just don't have the energy to take care of more stuff. Years ago I told my kids, don't bother giving me a gift unless I can eat it or drink it. There comes a point where it's all about letting loose of stuff—both physical and emotional baggage—not collecting more." (Brenda Bottoms, 60)

"I am 62 and I think I am 'more frugal' out of both necessity and volunteering to not waste as much. I am on a fixed income; it does not go far. I retired early, because of a layoff after 25 years and a shortage of jobs with a livable wage and benefits. I think with the passage of time, one realizes how wasteful they have been, of their time, money, and material goods. I want to leave a good world behind for my children and grandchildren. I want there to be plenty of water and land and fresh air for them. So it isn't just about money, it is being thrifty with using things. I walk when I can, I reuse plastics, I try to grow what food I can." (Anonymous)

"Dunno if I got more frugal—I think I just got SMARTER." (Evelyn Edgett, 55)

A SIMPLE LOOK AT RETIREMENT PLANNING EVEN A CHEAPSKATE CAN AGREE WITH

This simple self-assessment of how you stand as you look toward retirement is compliments of my colleagues at AARP and is used in a webinar on retirement planning I occasionally participate in presenting for AARP members.

- Can your guaranteed income cover both your fixed and variable expenses? If yes, you're in good shape.

- If not, can your guaranteed income cover at least your fixed expenses? If yes, vary your other expenses based upon how your investments perform.

- If not, can your guaranteed *and* variable income cover your fixed and variable expenses? If yes, figure out ways to cut costs as much as possible and leave some savings for emergencies.

- Can your guaranteed *and* variable income cover at least your fixed expenses? If yes, eliminate any nonessential items, cut costs as much as possible, and consider working part-time in retirement or delaying retirement to increase savings and maximize Social Security benefits. If not, check to see if you are eligible for any other social services benefits and delay retirement if possible to increase savings and maximize Social Security benefits.

LYS AND DAN BURDEN

Lifting Off to Retirement

"House levitation" was not a concept I was familiar with before I spoke with Lys and Dan Burden, who live in Port Townsend, Washington. Actually, at the time, they were living about twenty feet *above* Port Townsend, Washington. You might say their housing situation was "up in the air."

Lys, sixty-five, and Dan, sixty-eight, are preparing for their retirement years in a rather unusual way: They're "levitating"—yes, raising off the ground—the single-story, 1889 Victorian-era house they bought in 2005. Underneath the house they'll then construct a nine-hundred-square-foot fully equipped apartment and a four-hundred-square-foot guest unit, all within the footprint of the original house. In their retirement, they'll have the option of living in "the main house" and renting out the apartment, or the other way around. Dan estimates the apartment would rent for about $700 per month, while the original part of the house would bring in closer to $1,000 a month if they decide to rent that out instead.

"I think we'll treat ourselves to living in the original house once everything is finally finished," Lys says. "But as we grow older, at some point we'll downsize our possessions and move to the apartment downstairs, if for no other reason than to avoid the extra set of stairs."

The Burdens are part of a growing movement to create what are called "accessory dwelling units," or ADUs, adding a second, smaller residence onto—or in this case, underneath—an existing home. ADUs can also involve converting existing spaces, like basements, attics, and garages, into residential units. The ADU movement is just that—a true "movement," because it's about a lot more than just "duplexifying" (my own make-believe word!) the nation's neighborhoods.

"It's all about retrofitting and revitalizing and reenergizing existing residential areas," Dan says. "It's about making our communities more accessible, livable, and vibrant, rather than continuing the trend toward abandoning them or building more and more nonsustainable new developments in the outskirts. Ultimately it's about using the space we already have, but using it smarter and living lighter on the planet."

Dan also points out that increasing the population within existing residential areas pumps up the community's tax base, allowing municipalities to better maintain parks, streets, and other public services and projects. "If enough retired and other folks were to go the ADU route, it would make a tremendous difference both for their own personal finances and the financing of better communities, where they live," he says. Of course, not all municipalities have zoning laws that allow for ADUs, although, according to Dan, many communities across the country are realizing the benefits of the ADU movement and changing their zoning regulations to allow and encourage such facilities.

But levitating their home to create an ADU is only one of the tricks the Burdens have up their sleeves in terms of planning for their retirement years. The couple benefited from Dan's years of business travel, which allowed him to scope out locations all across the country as possible affordable and otherwise idealistic retirement spots. It's not hard to understand why they settled on Port Townsend. The postcard-pretty town of about nine thousand sits on a point jetting out into Puget Sound and is alive with recreational and cultural activities of every variety. And if this peaceful backwater ever starts feeling a little too peaceful, Seattle is only forty miles away.

"It really has everything we were looking for," Lys says. "It's rare to find so much diversity in a small town, and the sense of community is amazing. It even hosts its own annual kinetic sculpture races!" (Me: clueless expression.)

"Just Google it, Jeff!" she laughs. I subsequently did, and you should too.

Very high on the Burdens' list of prerequisites for potential retirement locales was a place where they could live "car-lite" or even entirely "car-free." That's not surprising since Dan is the cofounder and executive director of the Walkable and Livable Communities Institute (www.walk live.org), a nonprofit organization dedicated to "working to create healthy, connected communities that support active living and that advance opportunities for all people through walkable streets, livable cities and better built environments."

"Port Townsend is going to allow us to make ample use of our legs and lungs," Dan says. He calculates that they'll save at least $11,500 per year by living in a place where they don't need to own a car—let alone two or three, as the average American family does today. The Burdens currently share a car with Lys's brother, who also lives in Port Townsend, and the area has an excellent public bus system that allows them to get to Seattle for a mere $12 round-trip. Of course, around town, they prefer walking or bicycling, and Lys is quick to credit those money-saving athletic activities for her loss of twenty-five pounds within the first year of moving to Port Townsend. "You can't help getting healthier when you live here," she says.

Dan is a soft-spoken, openly compassionate man, with a wild and wonderfully bushy mustache and rather longish gray hair flanking a hairline that has seriously receded with the years. I think to myself, *Who does he remind me of?* And then I realize that in fifteen years or so, if I'm fortunate enough, I'll probably look exactly like Dan Burden—cheapskate brothers, born a generation apart? His incredible personal stories of worldwide adventuring and caring for the health of the planet make me worship him all the more. Somehow our shared receding hairlines and overgrown mustaches become a proud band of budget-minded brotherhood.

Lys is clearly Dan's soul mate, to use a popular term from the era when the couple first met during a caving trip in Kentucky in 1965, and at least his equal when it comes to having a passion for life and adventure. Before the couple married in 1970, Lys and two of her girlfriends spent a year hitchhiking around Europe—all the way to Istanbul—and eventually ended up living on a kibbutz in Israel. "Hey, where else could we live and eat for free?" she says with a chuckle.

"Lys and I have had a lot of practice preparing to do this," Dan says, referring to both their current creative housing project and their plans to retire the cheapskate way. "When we lived in the early '70's as 'almost hippies' in Missoula (Montana), we bought our own house in a very nice neighborhood by assuming someone else's mortgage and selling shares to friends and family in order to raise the $17,000 we needed to buy out the owner's mortgage."

"Shareholders" in the Burdens' home had the option of living in one of the home's five bedrooms at the rock-bottom rental rate of $30 per month. That allowed Dan and Lys to make the monthly mortgage payments and build equity in the home, all while enjoying essentially a free place to live while they both attended the University of Montana. When the couple moved to Florida nine years later, they sold the house and managed to repay each of the shareholders twice the amount each had "invested."

"At that time we were considered well below the poverty line, but we lived like kings and queens," Dan says. "We were living car-free and eating really healthy by buying in bulk for everyone living in the house. It worked out to about $30 per person per month for all of our food. So for a total of $60 a month, including utilities, everyone was getting room and board, while their original investment in the house was growing. Not bad, eh?" In fact, the Burdens were such pioneers in living a good life on less that, in 1974, *Money* magazine featured them in an article about alternative lifestyle choices and how to get the most out of the money you have to work with.

The Burdens had their first child, Jodi, in 1977, and their second, Juli, was born in 1984 after they moved to Tallahassee. Dan became a transportation planner for the state of Florida, and Lys founded and ran a number of recreation-related nonprofit organizations. Although the Burdens have always lived adventuresome lives, Lys says that raising their two daughters was one of their biggest adventures of all.

"We were living a pretty simple life, as we always have, and that's how our daughters were raised," she says. "They never demanded a lot of stuff, unlike many of their friends, because that wasn't how we lived." But that's not to say that the Burdens' daughters were deprived of any of the things that Dan and Lys themselves valued in life—just the opposite. The girls traveled widely with their parents, from bicycling through Europe to canoeing the rivers of Florida to hiking trails far and wide. The Burden family was constantly going, and doing, and seeing. Today, Jodi still lives in Florida with her husband and the Burdens' first grandchild, Jackson, and Juli lives in Hawaii, where she will attend the University of Hawaii in Honolulu.

Having cashed in most of their retirement savings to buy and remodel their home and ADU in Port Townsend, the Burdens will have a relatively modest income during their retirement years, relying mostly on Social Security, income from their rental unit, and a small pension from Dan's job at the Florida Department of Transportation. And both of the Burdens plan to continue to generate some income through selfish employment ventures of their own. Dan intends to transition in his work to more of a teaching role and less consulting—and less traveling. Lys hopes to write a series of young people's eco-adventure books, which she describes as "Harry Potter, but rather than battling monsters and evil wizards, the struggle these kids and their town will have is how to transition from the world of today to the sustainable world of tomorrow." To further supplement their income— and provide Lys with firsthand experience for her writing— the Burdens plan to raise most or even all of their own food, including chickens and eggs, on their property and in the

growing number of community gardens sprouting up around
Port Townsend.

For a couple who have spent their whole lives finding
creative ways to get the most out of life while spending less
and living lighter on the planet, Dan and Lys Burdens' retirement years promise to be an enjoyable continuation of
their lifelong adventure together, levitated house and all.

CHAPTER 4

50 Simple Ways to Feather Your Retirement Nest Egg

I f you're an average American consumer, guess how much you could save for retirement if you did any one of the following:

- Drink tap water instead of bottled water for the next eighteen months, assuming that you currently drink only bottled water to get your daily recommended intake of H_2O.
- Cancel your family of four's newspaper and magazine subscriptions for one year and read them online instead, and also borrow from the public library all movies, music, and books—including this one (I'm no hypocrite!)—you'd normally pay for during that year.
- Adopt for free—rather than purchase—any dogs or cats that you're likely to own over the next fifteen years.
- Dine out (including restaurant meals as well as carry-out/fast food) only half as much this year as your family of four does in a typical year, and instead cook those meals at home.

- For two years: Keep your house three degrees colder in the winter, three degrees warmer in the summer, and install an automatic timer to turn your hot-water heater on and off during periods when it's not normally in use.
- If you drive your kids to school every day and act as their personal chauffeur for all extracurricular activities, have them ride the school bus for at least one year and arrange carpools with other parents so that you're not doing all the after-school driving yourself.
- And finally, if you do any of the following, just stop doing it for one year: smoke one or more packs of cigarettes a day; buy six or more lottery tickets per day; drink one or more alcoholic beverages per day at a bar/restaurant; eat at least one candy bar, bag of chips, and soda purchased from a vending machine every day. (This savings tip is in tribute to actor Errol Flynn, who famously said in reference to his frequently freewheeling lifestyle, "My problem lies in reconciling my gross habits with my net income.")

Based on my calculations (e-mail me for the calculation details—UltCheapskate@aol.com), any one of the above cost-cutting measures will likely save you at least $2,000 during the time period indicated—money you could instead be putting into your retirement savings account.

I know what you're thinking: *Big whoop, cheapskate! You just told us that most financial experts think we should sock away a **million bucks** or more for retirement. What's two* *measly grand? I think I'll just keep ordering my kids their Happy Meals and be happy myself instead, thank you very much!*

Well, here's another way to look at it that might give you pause to reconsider: According to 2010 data from the US Census Bureau, half of all Americans have $2,000 or less saved for their retirement. Heck, I bet if you just visited a couple of financial planners every year and resold the empty Big Binders they give you on eBay, you could come up with more than $2,000 by the time you retire.

There's a popular saying among cheapskates: "If you pinch the pennies, the dollars will pinch themselves." Even the smallest savings—particularly on recurring expenses like some of those mentioned above—really add up over time. At the same time, literally saving even a single penny (or bending over to pick up a loose one on the sidewalk!) helps to instill in you what I call "the Ethic of Thrift," an attitude that makes wasting *any* amount of money that much more difficult.

With that in mind, here's a laundry list of ways to start setting aside more money for retirement by saving on everything from insurance to, well, laundry:

Around the House

- **Kill the dusty bunnies.** You may already know that regularly cleaning or replacing the filters on your furnace and air conditioner can save you up to 15 percent on those expensive-to-operate appliances (per the US Department of Energy—www.Energy.gov), but did you know that the dust bunnies hiding among the coils underneath your refrigerator are significantly reducing that appliance's energy efficiency as well? To clean, unplug the refrigerator or turn off the power to it. Gaining access to the coils varies by model; some can be accessed from the front and some only from the back. You may need to remove a plate covering the coils. Use an appropriate vacuum attachment or a brush to remove the dust, and wipe the coils off with soapy water if they're gummy.

- **Some other bright money- and energy-saving ideas.** We all know that CFLs (compact fluorescent lamps)— those new crazy corkscrew lightbulbs—are better for the environment because they use less energy. But I still think most people don't appreciate how much better they are for your wallet. Sure, they cost more to purchase, but because they last five to ten times longer than old-fashioned incandescent bulbs—and use 75 percent less electricity—you'll still have a *net savings* of about $10 per year for every frequently used incandescent bulb you replace with a CFL. And when it comes to simple ways to save electricity around the house, many appliances continue to use electricity even when they're turned off. Things like your TV, DVD player, stereo, cell phone charger, computer, and micro-wave oven—in general, electrical appliances with a standby mode or one of those square transformer-type plugs—are electrical vampires, accounting for 5 to 10 percent of your household's total electricity costs during the periods when they're *not* in use. Unplug them or, for greater convenience, attach multiple appliances to a single power strip that can easily be flipped off and on—it'll save you about $150 per year in electricity.

• **More wear and less tear from your clothing.** Making your clothes last twice as long—which you can easily do through a few simple tricks—could save the typical American family hundreds of dollar per year. A few ways to get more life out of your thrifty threads:

   ➤ Launder clothes less often, and only in cold water.

   ➤ Zip up metal zippers on jeans and jackets before laundering, because the zippers tear apart other garments in the wash.

   ➤ Turn bold prints and dark-colored garments inside out before laundering to keep colors from fading.

   ➤ Buy classic fashions—not fad styles—and maintain your body weight so they'll still be looking stylish and good on you ten years from now.

   ➤ Dry your clothes whenever possible on an old-fashioned clothesline instead of in an electric dryer; that alone will save you about $200 per year in the electricity/operating costs of an electric dryer and will make many garments last up to 50 percent longer.

In the Car

- **Gas-saving tips you may not know.** When it comes to increasing the fuel efficiency of your car, everyone knows that keeping your tires properly inflated, removing excess weight from the vehicle/trunk, and driving within the speed limit and less aggressively can make a big difference. But here are some things you may not know: Failing to fully twist the gas cap until it "clicks" after you fill up—or having an improperly fitting cap or no cap at all—can reduce your car's fuel efficiency by up to 10 percent. Also, in the summer heat, it pays to park in the shade whenever possible, both to save on cost by not making your air conditioner work so hard (cranking up the AC can reduce fuel efficiency by 10 to 20 percent) and to reduce the evaporation rate of gas in the engine. And here's an Ultimate Cheapskate special tip: after filling your tank—once the pump shuts off—tip the nozzle upside down, 180 degrees, and you'll drain a few extra ounces of gas that you've already paid for into your tank. Who knew?

- **Consider renting for long, quick trips.** If you do some simple math, you might find that in the long run you can sometimes save big money by leaving your wheels parked at home and renting a car instead. This is particularly true when it comes to trips where you'll be covering a lot of miles in a short period of time. Just take the price you paid for your car and divide it by the total number of miles you expect to drive it during the time you own it (sure, factor in any finance charges and possible resale value if you want to get fancy), to get a cost-per-mile that you can compare to the cost of renting a car for a specific trip. Often in the case of cars purchased new, this works out to twenty cents or more per mile. With rental car rates increasingly competitive—usually including unlimited free miles—on trips when you'll be driving more than a couple of hundred miles per day, it usually pays to rent. In urban areas, check out car-sharing programs like Zipcar (www.ZipCar.com) for potentially even greater savings. And, remember, the insurance you carry on your own car frequently covers you for rental vehicles, too, so no need to pay extra for the coverage offered by the rental company (check with your insurance agent just to be sure).

☞ *You might need a Cheapskate Intervention if you complain about the high cost of gas while waiting in line in your SUV to go through the drive-thru at McDonald's.*

• **Carefully consider the cost of your commute.** When most people go to buy a house or rent an apartment, sure, they think about what the commute will be like to their place of work. But most often they think of the commute primarily in terms of "how long" it will be, and less—if at all—about "how much" that commute will cost them over time. When you do the math, the cost (and potential *cost savings*) of a longer versus a shorter commute can be staggering. As an example, based on AAA estimates of the cost of owning/ operating the average vehicle and the average length of the American work commute (now around thirty-two miles round-trip per workday!), if you were to live close enough to your place of work so that you could walk or bicycle there every day instead of drive, you would save about $4,000 per year—and that's assuming that you still owned a car but just didn't use it to commute to/from work. If you took that savings and invested it at a 5 percent annual rate of return, after a forty-year career you would have a retirement nest egg of about $535,000, all just by choosing to live close to where you work.

Cheapskate Retirement Principle #6

Never underestimate the power of saving even a single penny. Every act of frugality—no matter how small— instills in you an "Ethic of Thrift" that makes wasting any amount of money that much harder. That's how to retire the cheapskate way.

Smart Shopping and Saving

- **Retire a monthly bill and retire that much sooner.** Nothing feels better (well, at least financially speaking) than making that last car payment or that last payment on your student loans or the kids' braces. And finally paying off your credit card—the one with the sushi dinner you ate back in 1989 still on it—or, Lord willing, your home mortgage, those are milestones you'll never forget. That's the point: DON'T forget such milestones. In fact, DON'T stop paying those bills, even when you can. Pay your savings/retirement account that same amount instead. After all, you've built the payment into your monthly budget; it's part of your normal financial routine, so bank it instead of spend it. This is another one of the little financial tricks my buddy Bob Johnson taught me, a sort of new twist on the old principle of "paying yourself first" when it comes to setting aside savings.

- **Always check the sales receipt.** Studies by the research firm A.T. Kearney and others have shown that across all retail purchases, nearly 30 percent of the time customers are charged an incorrect amount for at least one item among those items they are buying. This happens most frequently on items that are on sale, which is particularly frustrating to cheapskates—we go to great lengths to find a bargain, only to have to convince the cashier at the checkout stand of the sale price. It pays to review all receipts carefully before leaving the store, particularly since some grocery stores have a policy that if an item rings up at the wrong price, you get that item for free. And it also pays to be an honest cheapskate: In part to prove that my mind is still more efficient than any computerized inventory system ever invented, I once kindly pointed out to a cashier at the supermarket that the dozen eggs I was buying rang up at 20 cents *less* than the actual price. To my surprise and delight, I was rewarded for my honesty by being given the eggs for free, as the store's "accurate pricing guarantee" applied regardless of whether you were overcharged or undercharged.

• **Find the best FOP for *you*.** There's great debate within the cheapskate community about the best Form of Payment (or "FOP") when it comes to saving money. One school is adamant in its belief that if you always pay in cash, you'll end up spending a lot less and obviously reduce the risk of going into debt. There's a lot of research to support that position, including a recent Bankrate.com study that showed that customers who used a charge card to pay for their orders at fast-food restaurants ended up spending almost 50 percent more than those who paid in cash, likely supersizing both their waistlines and their credit card debt. But other frugal folks claim the best method is to use a cash-back credit card to make virtually all purchases, and religiously pay off the entire balance every month to avoid finance charges. This approach can certainly pay off *if* you have the discipline to pay off your charges every month and to avoid "plastic temptation"— the tendency to buy things you wouldn't otherwise buy because it's so easy to just "charge it." A number of cash-back credit cards offer 1 percent back on all purchases (even more on selected types of purchases); card offers change constantly, but currently three of the better cash-back credit cards worth checking out are Chase Freedom Visa, American Express's Blue Cash Preferred, and the TrueEarnings Card from Costco and American Express. Another simple way to set aside a little money for retirement is to enroll in one of the "round-up" debit card programs offered by many banks (including Bank of America), whereby every time you use your debit card for a purchase, the bank "rounds up" your purchase to the next whole dollar and automatically transfers that amount to your savings or money market account—it's like the twenty-first-century version of the spare-change jar on the bedroom dresser.

- **Lose a few pounds and save a few dollars.** "I go on a diet at least three or four times a year," Miser Adviser Rhonda Jones told me. Desserts are her biggest weakness, she confessed. "My dream date would be with Will Smith and Red Velvet cake . . . and if Will can't make it, I'll still be happy." Like most people, Rhonda dreaded her periodic exercises in taking off a few pounds, but when she realized that she was saving some pretty decent money during those diets, it became a little easier. "What I started doing was putting some cash in an envelope (about the cost of a slice of Red Velvet cake) whenever I was dieting and resisted my temptation to pig out." The results shocked her and inspired her to lose—and save—even more. "The first time I did it, I told myself I wouldn't count the money until I'd lost all the weight I wanted." After dieting/ saving for nearly a month, Rhonda counted the cash in the envelope and couldn't believe what she found: nearly $200 that otherwise, she says, "would have been on my thighs."

☞ *You might need a Cheapskate Intervention if you forget to thaw the turkey for Thanksgiving because you're too busy making your shopping list for Black Friday.*

- **Saver's Tax Credit—getting paid to save:** Having a modest income can have its advantages when it comes to building your retirement nest egg. Well, at least one, that's for sure. The often overlooked "Saver's Credit" (aka the "Credit for Qualified Retirement Savings Contributions") is specifically designed to encourage individuals and families with lower incomes to set aside some savings for retirement. The requirements are a little complicated, depending on your income and filing status, but basically if you put money into a 401(k), 403(b), IRA, or 457 plan, the federal government will in essence match your money by as much as 50 percent, up to a maximum of $1,000, if you qualify. So that $2,000 you managed to save through any of the penny-pinching methods described here could morph into $3,000. If you save less or your income is higher, your tax credit will be less. If your adjusted gross income exceeds a certain level (for 2011: $28,250 for single filers, $42,375 for head of household, $56,500 for married filing jointly), you won't be eligible. All the details are explained at www.irs.gov/form8880. Since it's a tax credit, you need to claim it (i.e., you don't automatically receive it), and an estimated 90 percent of people who could qualify don't take advantage of it.

• **Timing is everything.** It's possible to save megabucks to put toward your retirement simply by studying up on *when* is the best time to get the best deal on the services and goods you want. Research an industry's traditional slow times and offer to schedule your work during those periods—in exchange for a healthy discount. For example:

- Mid-weeks are slower for many auto mechanics.
- Tree services are often hurting for work in the wintertime.
- Get married between November and April.
- Schedule exterior home repairs in the fall and winter, and interior jobs in the spring and summer.
- Consider filing an extension on your taxes to take advantage of downtime in the tax and accounting industries.
- Business hotels are more prone to haggle on weekend rates.
- Get your lawnmower tuned up in the winter, your chimney swept in the summer, and your carpets cleaned *after* the holidays for the best chance at negotiating a better price.
- If you need your piano tuned, avoid the back-to-school rush in the fall and church holidays when you go to make your perfect pitch and ask for a discount.

There's an excellent book about the optimum times to do and buy just about everything, called *Buy Ketchup in May and Fly at Noon: A Guide to the Best Time to Buy This, Do That and Go There,* by Mark Di Vincenzo.

Cheapskate Retirement Principle #7

The most powerful way to turn small savings into big savings is to identify incremental ways to save on an ongoing, routine basis—changes that you can make in your life that, after they're in place, you don't need to think about again. For example, switching to a bank with lower fees or more convenient ATM locations, or switching brands of some of the products you use most often to less expensive store or generic brands. Set these simple savings plans in motion, and then forget about them.

Other Penny-Pinching Pointers

- **Shop for airline tickets about six weeks before you travel.** That's the advice from the Airlines Reporting Corporation (ARC) on when you're likely to get the best price on airline tickets. ARC is a company that accredits travel agencies and coordinates the sale of tickets and other travel services within the broader travel industry. While ARC's data suggest that six weeks out is the optimum time to find the best ticket prices, use that as a general guideline only, since special fares and other promotions may apply at other times as well. Also, try shopping for airline tickets on Tuesdays, since sale fares are usually launched on Monday nights and the following day competitors often rush to match them.

- **Buy generic meds for your pets.** I know something's wrong in the world when the medicines for the four feline hypochondriacs we share our house with cost more than the prescriptions for my wife and me. Of course, we buy generic drugs for ourselves whenever possible, and now you can do the same for your pets in many cases. An increasing number of national retailers—including Target and Kroger—and websites like www.royalpetmeds.com and www.onlinepetmeds .info offer generic versions of many common pet medicines at a fraction of the price of brand-name equivalents (in the case of Target, some generics are as little as $4). Check with your vet first to make sure that it's okay to substitute generics. Many pet stores now also carry a generic version of Frontline flea and tick protection.

- **Skip the service plans.** "Extended service plans" or "extended warranties" sold by many stores on appliances, electronics, and other items are a notoriously bad deal for the consumer in most cases. In fact it's been reported that they're used so infrequently once they're purchased that some stores make more profit— total—from the sale of service plans than they make from the sale of products themselves! Most often, either the item doesn't need to be repaired or replaced during the period covered by the plan, or if it does, by then the customer has forgotten ever buying the additional coverage and fails to pursue repair/replacement under the service plan. And, remember, most products come with a manufacturer's warranty that provides at least some recourse if an item is truly defective. Service plans typically cost 10 to 20 percent of the product's purchase price, sometimes even more. Cheapskates say that's money better invested in your retirement account instead.

☞ *You might need a Cheapskate Intervention if you need a shopping cart when shopping at 7-Eleven.*

- **Piggyback on your employer's phone plan.** If you have a cell phone and you're currently employed, be sure to check with your employer's phone company. Many companies—including Verizon, U.S. Cellular, T-Mobile, AT&T, and Sprint—often offer discounted cell phone plans (sometimes as high as 20 percent) to employees of their corporate customers. You can usually check for possible employee discounts on the carrier's website. And even if you're not employed but you volunteer for an organization such as a volunteer fire department, some phone companies offer discounts to volunteers who serve selected nonprofit groups.

Some Expenses to Lose in Retirement

Here are some simple ways to save once you are retired, so that you can lower your expenses and continue to build your nest egg even then:

- **Do you still need life insurance?** The answer to that question depends on your individual situation, but there's a good chance that as you grow older—particularly into your fifties and beyond—the need to continue to carry life insurance decreases. Especially if you have sufficient assets, are no longer working, and no longer have dependent children, continuing to carry life insurance may not make sense. That's because life insurance is typically used to prevent financial ruin if you should die during your working years and other people are dependent on that income. There are still instances when it may make sense to continue to carry life insurance once you're retired (e.g., you have a desire to leave the benefits to family members or charitable causes, or you're concerned about covering the costs of your funeral or outstanding debts upon your death), but in many cases it's an expense retirees can choose to lose. And that's particularly good news, since as you age, your life insurance premiums are likely to go up, up, up. A sixty-year-old male is probably paying about $1,600 per year for a $150,000 policy (about $1,200 for a sixty-year-old female), so if you can afford to drop it, the savings can be significant.

- **And you can probably also disable your disability insurance.** If you have disability insurance, once you've stopped working, the conventional wisdom is that it's probably a good idea to discontinue that coverage as well. Disability insurance is typically designed to replace some or all of your income if you become disabled and can no longer work, but once you're retired, that's not really an issue, is it? Disability premiums vary based on a number of factors (e.g., age, income, benefits, etc.). But a policy for a midcareer worker making $50,000 per year, for example, could easily cost $1,500 to $2,000 in annual premiums, depending on how much of the worker's income would be replaced in the event of disability. So it's a considerable savings opportunity once you're retired.

- **Lose higher auto insurance premiums.** In Chapter 6, we'll look more closely at "simple-sizing" your transportation needs in retirement, but even if you decide to hang on to your own wheels once you're retired, there are a couple of easy ways you might be able to reduce your auto insurance premiums. If you're driving less because you no longer commute to work, in many states you can cut your insurance rates by having a device installed in your car that verifies your lower mileage and safe driving habits; check with your insurance company to see if this program is available. And you may be able to save up to 10 percent on your auto policy if you complete AARP's Driver Safety course. That could be a savings of about $80 per year based on national averages. AARP offers both classroom and online versions of this popular course, with registration fees averaging in the $15 to $20 range. Restrictions may apply, so ask your insurance agent about it before you sign up, although it's a useful and kind of fun refresher course regardless. For more info, see www.aarp.org/drive.

SAVING YOUR AGE

Here's a fun approach to setting aside money for retirement, compliments of one of my Miser Advisers: Try "Saving Your Age," plus two zeros, every year.

So, for example, when you're twenty, your goal is to set aside at least $2,000 for retirement that year, and then $2,100 the next year, when you're twenty-one, and so on. According to Charlie Fischer, the cheapskate genius who came up with the idea, it has worked well for him for many years, and now that his daughter is working, she's enrolled in Charlie's "Saving Your Age" program too.

"I know it sounds silly, and it's totally arbitrary and may not work for everyone," Charlie admits, "but it's been an easy way for me to think about and remember how much I plan to put away for retirement every year . . . as long as I can remember how old I am, that is." To simplify things, Charlie has authorized his bank to automatically transfer the desired amount from his checking/general account into his retirement investment account according to a preset monthly schedule.

Charlie has also found that the gradual escalation of increasing his annual retirement saving by only $100 every year has been virtually painless, but mathematically it really adds up: assuming, say, a 5 percent annual rate of return, Charlie's "Saving Your Age" program will generate a retirement nest egg of nearly $500,000 over the course of a forty-year career.

If you can't free up your age plus two zeros to set aside for retirement every year, try just banking your age every week (e.g., $21 per week when you're twenty-one years old). It's easier than you think, particularly since your salary is likely to increase steadily throughout your career, making the weekly set-asides that much less noticeable. You'll be saving only about half as much under this modified "Saving Your Age" plan, but a quarter of a million dollars in the bank after a forty-year career ain't nothin' to sneeze at either.

STACIE BARNETT
(above, with T.J.)

—▬ ▬—

A Born-Again Cheapskate

"A s soon as I was old enough to understand what it meant to be retired, I knew that's what I wanted to be when I grew up."

Stacie Barnett is a thirty-two-year-old single mom living with her twelve-year-old son, T.J., in two rooms of her parent's ranch-style home in Batavia, Illinois. Although technically a suburb of Chicago, Batavia very much has the feel of a small midwestern town all its own, with the placid Fox River flowing lazily through the center of town.

The story of how this attractive administrative assistant working at a local union office ended up moving back in with her parents a couple of years ago is sad, although not that uncommon these days.

What is uncommon, though, is the overflowing optimism and sense of purpose that Stacie has about her future. Chief among her plans: making her lifelong retirement dreams a reality in the not-too-distant future, something that at her lowest point just a few years ago she had written off like a bounced check.

It's a cliché to say that someone has a "winning personality," but in Stacie's case, if anything, it's an understatement. Her easy laugh, mischievous smile, and Amy Adams good looks are only part of her arsenal of charm. It's immediately apparent that she has a mind every bit as sharp as her wit, and we're talking Ginsu knife kind of sharp. Ouch!

Given all that she's obviously got going for her, I'm all the more curious to hear her story of how she came to be living where she's living now and, even more so, why she seems so hot-diggity-dog upbeat about what the future holds for her and T.J.

"It wasn't until I entered the workforce that I realized that retirement wasn't something that was automatically handed to you just because you managed to survive until your golden years," she says, reflecting on her first civilian job after serving for a year in the navy and her brief marriage ending in divorce. At that time, she had just started working as a buyer for a chain of salon spas in the Midwest, and the future looked pretty bright. "I realized that retirement had to be earned. Since retirement had always been my dream job, I decided to be vigilant in my quest for financial independence.

"I began contributing the maximum amount I could towards my 401(k) right from the start . . . not an easy thing to do for a young single mom who wasn't making very much money at the time. I was really, really careful with my money, watching every penny I spent and saving everything I could," she says with a rightful sense of pride and accomplishment. "I also started reading books like *Rich Dad, Poor Dad* and *Rich Dad's Retire Young, Retire Rich.*" She then quickly adds with a little laugh: "Apparently I enjoyed books with commas in the title back then. I also took *every* real estate investing course I could find. Robert Kiyosaki's, Robert Allen's . . . if your name was Robert, and you peddled investment classes, you most likely went on vacation with my money during that period in my life."

As Stacie is telling me all of this, my imagination keeps jumping ahead. I'm trying to imagine the circumstances that brought this remarkably bright, obviously responsible young woman down. Down to the point of moving back into the very same bedroom in her parents' home she'd called her own as a young girl.

What she tells me next may seem counterintuitive, but I've heard it—and even experienced shades of it myself—before.

"And then I started making more money. Lots and lots of money, in fact. And then I started making money mistakes.

Lots and lots of money mistakes. It was like my new big pay-checks had completely unraveled every logical and sensible thing I knew about money management." As she talks about it, you can see that it's still very painful for her to recall. For the first time, she seems less composed and self-assured. "With only a high school degree, I never expected to have a big job, making big money, and I convinced myself that being successful was about making and spending it as fast as you could. It was a high-stress job, and so I felt I deserved to live a high-class lifestyle."

There was a brand-new car; a time-share property in Branson, Missouri; and a condo purchased at the peak of the run-up in the housing market. "I think the bubble burst the day after I closed on my condo," she says. Stacie's spending just continued to escalate, and even though she was making more than she had ever made—or ever imagined that she'd make—for the first time in her adult life, she wasn't able to set aside anything at all in savings. "That's crazy, isn't it?" she says with a sad shake of her head.

All of that was bad enough—and foolish—Stacie admits, but little did she realize that the perfect storm was about to strike. "Then the market crashed. The company I worked for took a big hit, and suddenly I was being pulled into an office and told that they would be cutting my big paycheck in half. I had started that day making $50,000 a year. By the end of the day, I was making $25,000 . . . and in the course of two years I had managed to get myself into $165,000 of debt, including more than $30,000 just in credit cards.

I cashed out the entire amount of my 401(k) just to make a dent in my mountain of debt and keep my head above water. My dream of retirement became a nightmare."

Now with two mortgages on her condo (she took out a second in an attempt to stay afloat) and one for her time-share, barely able to make even the minimum payments on her credit cards, Stacie realized that she needed to rediscover her Inner Cheapskate. She needed to "get defensive about (her) finances again," the way she'd been before her big paychecks caused her to contract a severe case of Debtor Dementia. (FYI: "Debtor Dementia" or, in Latin, *Insaneous Borrowlingus*, is a condition I first diagnosed years ago, a delusional state that otherwise rational people enter once they begin borrowing money. A common symptom is that they start using phrases like "good debt" and "leveraged financing." The hopeful news is that, with proper Cheapskate Interventions, Debtor Dementia is curable in most patients.)

"That's why I consider myself a born-again cheapskate," Stacie says, with her smile now back in full force. "And thankfully, I'm well on my way to a full financial recovery."

Stacie's parents, Pete and Pam, were aware of and concerned about their daughter's dire financial situation. "At the time, I felt like a total failure," Stacie says. "I just felt so guilty and ashamed." When her parents reminded her that she and T.J. were always welcome to move in with them, Stacie swallowed hard and knew what she needed to do.

"I was excited about them moving in," Pete, Stacie's dad, says about the relocation. "I did not like them living so far away, but at the same time I was disappointed that Stacie couldn't make it financially because of a terrible economy that affected her profession at that time. Someday it will be nice to be an empty nester, but not now." Stacie's mom adds, "There are a lot of adult children moving back in with their parents these days. And while I feel that, as a parent, it's your duty to help your children, I also think it's important that they contribute to the household expenses and pull their weight around the house." Since moving back in with her folks, Stacie has been paying them $300 per month in rent and utilities and also buying all the food for herself and T.J. "It's really worked out pretty well for all of us, as awful as I felt about it at first," she says.

Fortunately Stacie was able to sell her condo and actually walk away from the deal with about $2,000 in her pocket. Without the two mortgage payments on her condo hanging over her head, Stacie focused like a cheapskate on steroids (generic brand, of course) on paying off her other debts. The $30,000 in credit card debt: all gone. The car loan: paid in full. And this year she'll make the final payment on her time-share property, which she decided to hang on to for a variety of reasons. She's also once again been able to start building up a small savings/retirement account and emergency fund.

The other big news is that Stacie has gone back to school to get the college degree in business administration she regrets not getting years ago. We share a good cheapskate laugh when I ask how much she'll be borrowing in student loans to finance her somewhat belated college education. "Not a dime! It's all pay-as-I-go!" she says.

Stacie has been attending evening classes at a local community college, where she'll graduate with an associate's degree in spring 2013. Then she'll complete the course work for her bachelor's degree at nearby Aurora University, which also offers special evening classes for nontraditional students. (Just to clarify, Stacie is classified as a "nontraditional student" because she's a little older and works full-time, *not* because she's a born-again cheapskate. While cheapskate discrimination is quite common, Aurora University is not an offender.) Stacie also hopes to be able to help T.J. financially if he chooses to go to college, although she's already steering him toward the affordable community-college/live-at-home type of plan she's using herself.

As for Stacie's reconstituted retirement strategy, it sounds familiar. With the elimination of all her personal debt, Stacie hopes to buy a duplex in the next year, using a fifteen-year fixed-rate mortgage or refinancing to one as soon as possible. She and T.J. will live in one unit and rent out the other. If all goes as planned, she may also *carefully* invest in other rental properties as well (small, affordable units, ideal for single parents like herself), so that when she retires—which she still hopes will be in her fifties—she'll have three income streams to depend on: Social Security, 401(k), and rental income. And, of course, she's quick to add that the main lesson she's learned the hard way and will carry with her into retirement is "how much you spend is even more important than how much you earn."

"Do you think that's an insane plan, Jeff?" she asks. I issue my standard disclaimer about never advising people concerning their individual financial situations, although she's clearly interested and somewhat reassured when I tell her about how many frugal folks—including Denise and me—rely in part on rental properties to at least diversify their retirement income streams.

"I don't know. I could be totally crazy to think that this (her retirement plan) might work," she says with another of her mischievous little grins. "The great thing about being single is that I get to make all of my own financial decisions. The terrible thing about being single is that I have no one else to blame for all my financial mistakes. If I could give one piece of financial advice to single parents, it would be to always consult with someone you know who makes smart-money decisions in their own lives *before* you make any major money decisions."

But even if you have made some serious financial mistakes in the past and you are a "born-again cheapskate"—and particularly if your name is Stacie Barnett—I'll bet dollars to donuts that in the long run your financial successes are going to make your financial blunders look like a BB rolling down a four-lane highway. (How's that for mixing metaphors?)

CHAPTER 5

Can You Retire Comfortably on Social Security Alone?

Yeah, yeah, yeah, when it comes to Social Security, you've heard it all before:

- Six in ten nonretirees believe that Social Security will not be able to pay them benefits when they stop working; 56 percent of current retirees believe that their Social Security benefits will eventually be cut. (2010 *USA Today*/Gallup poll)

- "I was too old for a paper route, too young for Social Security, and too tired for an affair." (Erma Bombeck)

- In 1950, for every retiree receiving Social Security, 16 people were still working and paying into the system. By 2010, that had dropped to just 3.3 workers, and by 2025 it is projected to drop to just 2 workers for each retiree. (US Congressional Budget Office data)

- "I care about our young people, and I wish them great success, because they are our Hope for the Future, and some day, when my generation retires, they will have to pay us trillions of dollars in Social Security." (Dave Barry)

- If nothing changes, projected benefits will surpass earmarked revenues for entitlement programs, including Social Security and Medicare, by $46 trillion over the next 75 years. (US Government Accountability Office, 2009 data)

- "Social Security is a government program with a constituency made up of the old, the near old and those who hope or fear to grow old. After 215 years of trying, we have finally discovered a special interest that includes 100 percent of the population. Now we can vote ourselves rich." (P. J. O'Rourke)

- "We shall make the most lasting progress if we recognize that Social Security can furnish only a base upon which each one of our citizens may build his individual security through his own individual efforts." (Franklin D. Roosevelt)

- "We're entering an age when average Americans will live longer and live more productive lives. And these amendments adjust to that progress. The changes in this legislation will allow Social Security to age as gracefully as all of us hope to do ourselves, without becoming an overwhelming burden on generations still to come." (Ronald Reagan, signing the Social Security Amendments of 1983)

- "They want the federal government controlling Social

Security like it's some kind of federal program."
(George W. Bush)

- "In 2016 we will begin paying more in benefits than we collect in taxes. Without changes, by 2033 the Social Security Trust Fund will be exhausted and there will be enough money to pay only about 75 cents for each dollar of scheduled benefits. We need to resolve these issues soon to make sure Social Security continues to provide a foundation of protection for future generations." (The cautionary disclaimer now included in the online personal statement prepared by the Social Security Administration)

But when it comes to Social Security, what you may not have heard is this: Roughly 35 percent of recipients over the age of sixty-five rely *entirely* or *almost entirely* (i.e., at least 90 percent) on Social Security as their sole source of retirement income, according to the Employee Benefit Research Institute (www.ebri.org). And for 55 percent of elderly recipients, Social Security provides the majority of their income. Without Social Security benefits, nearly half of all Americans aged sixty-five or older would have incomes below the official US poverty line ($10,890/one person and $14,710/two-person family, per US Department of Health and Human Services 2011 statistics).

I admit that I was shocked—and deeply saddened—to learn these facts about Social Security. People often refer to Social Security as a "safety net," but the reality is, without that net in place, nearly half of those sixty-five and older would fall through into the abyss of poverty.

Of course, no one is suggesting that depending entirely on Social Security for your retirement income is a prudent thing to do, cheapskate or otherwise. From its very inception, Social Security was intended only to augment your income in retirement.

Although with employer-funded pension plans disappearing faster than twelve-packs of toilet paper off a store shelf in an episode of *Extreme Couponing*, and people's 401(k)s and other retirement savings being eaten alive in the stock market or vanishing overnight in the event of a medical or other emergency, many predict that dependency on Social Security (as a percentage of total income) will actually increase among the waves of baby boomers now retiring. This, just as the Social Security system itself faces one of the greatest fiscal challenges in its seventy-five-plus-year history.

"We believe that more and more people will be relying on Social Security for most or even all of their income as they enter retirement in the coming years," AARP's Jean Setzfand told me in an interview. "The elimination of traditional, defined benefit pension plans has put the onus on the employees to save for their own retirements, and in a lot of cases people have simply failed to save and have spent their money elsewhere instead. And of course with traditional pensions, the employer bore all the market risks . . . the retirement benefits were guaranteed to the employee regardless of what happened in the market. Now the employees make their own investment decisions and assume all the market risk."

With the monthly Social Security benefit for a retired worker averaging about $1,177 in 2011 (per the Social Security Administration)—or a little over $14,000 per year—I was curious to talk with my Miser Advisers about the practicality of living primarily or even exclusively on Social Security in retirement. As you'll see in some of their upcoming profiles, a number of my fellow cheapskates do indeed live largely on Social Security alone—sometimes out of necessity and sometimes out of choice—and their resulting lifestyles are pretty basic, but by no means joyless.

What struck me was that many of my fellow cheapskates have a condition I've now diagnosed as "Social Security Stretcher's Syndrome" (or "SSSS"), whereby they take tremendous personal pride in how far they can stretch their monthly Social Security checks, even if they have other income they could use to cover their expenses.

For many, like sixty-eight-year-old Anna Best and her circle of lady friends, it's almost become a competitive sport. "We get together every Wednesday to play pinochle, but we spend most of the time talking about how little we've spent the past week . . . all of the bargains and coupons we've found . . . and compare notes on how much of our Social Security money is left for the rest of the month. We always laugh about that song 'Too Much Month at the End of the Money,'" she says. Even though Anna and most of her friends have other income in addition to their Social Security benefits that they can tap, "It's become a little side game (comparing notes on their SSSS), and it really helps to keep us on our toes when it comes to pinching pennies."

Although, again, no responsible financial pundit would ever advise you that you should, by design, attempt to rely entirely on Social Security for your retirement income, a common practice among many cheapskates is to attempt to cover all of their fixed monthly expenses with their Social Security benefits. This seems to me to be a reasonable and good goal for many retirees. As we'll see, it involves both reducing those fixed expenses as much as possible and injecting yourself with the Social Security Stretcher's Syndrome virus so you can get the most out of your monthly checks.

Cheapskate Retirement Principle #8

NEVER PLAN to retire on your Social Security benefit alone—it's designed to replace only 30 to 40 percent of most people's preretirement income. **BUT DO PLAN** to maximize and stretch the amount of your Social Security benefit as much as possible, and work to reduce your fixed expenses so that ideally your monthly Social Security check will at least cover your routine monthly bills.

But How Secure Is Social Security?

- - - - - - - -

That question is of course a topic of great public debate, and the myriad answers you hear are reflective of the myriad sources anxious to opine on the topic.

Politicians of every stripe love to pontificate about the demise of Social Security as a reason to vote for them . . . even if they're openly opposed to doing anything about it. Financial planners—at least many commission-based advisers, those hoping to sell you more investment products—are quick to tell you that you shouldn't count on Social Security for much, if anything, regardless of how close you are to retirement. ("And oh, by the way, you need at least $1 million to retire!") Organizations like AARP that represent senior citizens obviously realize that Social Security's woes are a powerful tool for recruiting more supporters and donations. And even some members of the clergy apparently recognize Social Security's plight as a potential collection plate issue: the sign in front of a local church here in Maryland read, "JESUS: The Only Social Security You Can Depend On."

☞ *You might need a Cheapskate Intervention if you refuse to have an IRA because you don't believe in an independent Northern Ireland.*

While there's no shortage of opinions or legitimate reasons to be concerned over the long-term future of Social Security, the reality of the situation is probably a lot less dire than most Americans appear to think it is, at least as reflected in the 2010 *USA Today*/Gallup poll mentioned on page 116.

Fueled by all the political rhetoric, the public's pessimism over the survival of Social Security seems to be based in large part on a misunderstanding about the impact of the projected depletion of the Social Security trust fund by 2033. Keep in mind that the trust fund—all $2.6 trillion of it—consists of funds amassed since the mid-1980s, during a period in which Social Security collected more in taxes and other income each year than it paid out in benefits. Because of these surplus funds, according to the Social Security Administration, the program can continue to pay out full benefits through 2033, despite the fact that the balance has already shifted to the point where now every year more is paid out in Social Security benefits than is collected in new taxes and other income.

But there are two important things to keep in mind, and this is where the public confusion comes in about the oft predicted death of Social Security: (1) Even if the trust fund is eventually depleted, the program will still be able to continue to pay out benefits at about 75 percent of the current/full rate, simply by using annual tax revenues going forward. (2) This "worst case scenario"—a 25 percent reduction in your monthly Social Security check starting in about 2033—assumes that no action is taken to fix the problem before it actually happens.

"The public perception that Social Security is just going

to entirely disappear is incorrect," Jean Setzfand says, even though AARP acknowledges that adjustments are needed in order to ensure that workers will receive the benefits they are promised.

Let's Get 'Er Done

"Hell, nobody wants to take a 25 percent pay cut," Rob Harden told me when I asked about the possibility of a scaling back of future Social Security benefits in 2033. "But 75 percent is a hell of a lot better than zero percent. You know what the hell I'm sayin', Jeff?"

Harden, a widower, is a recently retired electrician now living in the Florida Panhandle. He could easily be a body double for Sergeant Carter on the old *Gomer Pyle, U.S.M.C.* show. While Rob doesn't rely entirely on Social Security for his income, he estimates that in a typical month it does account for "90 percent plus" of what he actually spends.

He clearly embraces and revels in his Social Security Stretcher's Syndrome. Among his arsenal of penny-pinching techniques, two of Rob's favorite pastimes—fishing and home brewing—nicely supplement his food budget. ("But Rob, is beer a food?" I naively asked. "Hell yes! Are you crazy?") One of his other hobbies is combing the popular beaches along the Gulf with the metal detector his kids gave him as a retirement gift. While his treasure hunting hasn't made him rich, he's proud to say that he always finds at least enough in lost change and trinkets to pay for the batteries necessary to keep his detector powered up. Plus with the sky-high price of gold today, the two class rings and the 14k gold chain he's unearthed over the past year could provide some serious mad money if he ever takes them out of his "booty box" and cashes them in. And economizing on the home front, a pair of unwanted solar panels Rob salvaged from a job site before he retired and installed on his 1950s bungalow has reduced his electric bill to near zilch.

In Rob's case, a 25 percent reduction in benefits would drop his monthly Social Security check to just under $900. That prospect makes him grimace, but he's quick to add, "Nine hundred bucks is still nine hundred bucks, and I ain't gonna stop cashing the checks because they're smaller." Rob has also befriended a number of local electrical contractors since he relocated to Florida and is confident that he could secure part-time employment through that network if he needs some extra income. For the time being, though, he much prefers the company of his fishing tackle box over his electrician's toolbox.

So while he has some options, at seventy-one, Harden believes that he won't live long enough to see the possible reduction of Social Security benefits in 2033. "Hell, my dad had been dead for three years by the time he was my age, if you know what the hell I mean." But as you might guess, Rob has strong feelings about the need to protect Social Security for future generations. "This is a hell of a great country we live in, and we need to do the right thing and fix it (the Social Security system)." Well said, Rob Harden, you hellion, you.

How can Social Security be "fixed" in order to prevent a 25 percent reduction in benefits, come 2033? The good news is there's no shortage of options. And that's the bad news, too. With so many possible solutions on both the revenue side (i.e., tax increases) and the spending side (i.e., benefit cuts), the debate smolders on.

Ultimately the fix—at least for the *next* seventy-five years of the program—may well involve a compromise, a mix of both revenue and spending adjustments. A 2010 report by the US Senate Special Committee on Aging presented a cogent, even mildly comforting assessment of possible solutions. In fact, at the time, the chairman of that committee, Senator Herb Kohl (D-Wisconsin), told the Associated Press, "Modest changes can be made over time that will keep the program in surplus. They are not draconian, as the report points out, and they can be done and will be done." He even went on to describe the necessary changes as mere "tweaks" of the current system.

☞ *You might need a Cheapskate Intervention if you've never used your employer's cafeteria plan because you can't figure out which floor of the building the cafeteria is on.*

Possible revenue-side solutions identified by the committee included a payroll tax increase of 1.1 percentage points for both workers and employers, or starting to tax all wages, not just those below $110,100.* Either of those actions by themselves would allow the program to continue to pay full benefits going forward.

In terms of possible adjustments to benefits, the committee reported that three-fourths of the projected shortfalls over the next seventy-five years could be eliminated if the annual cost-of-living increases were reduced by 1 percent each year. Currently, Social Security recipients get annual increases based on the rate of inflation. The remaining gap could essentially be closed by gradually increasing the age when retirees qualify for full benefits from sixty-seven to sixty-eight. Clearly, possible benefit changes like these, although relatively modest in comparison to the scope of the entire program, can have a profound impact on individuals and their specific retirement plans; they will need to be monitored and considered carefully in your retirement planning should they become law.

Whether you consider possible solutions like these "draconian," "tweaks," or perhaps draconian tweaks, I like Rob Harden's attitude: we're a hell of a great nation, and we need to do what's right and fix Social Security.

---

*Currently, wages in excess of $110,100 are exempt from Social Security tax. That's something that many Americans don't even realize, perhaps because the average annual wage in the United States is only about $42,000, 100 percent of which is subject to Social Security withholding.

8 Cheapskate Keys to Surviving—and *Maybe* Even Thriving—on Social Security Alone

Fair enough, I know what you're thinking. The title of this chapter is "Can You Retire Comfortably on Social Security Alone?" but I haven't really answered that question. Alright, the answer I've come up with is this: **Maybe, but probably only if you can really afford not to.**

Here's what I mean by that, based on the current Social Security system and benefits and conversations with my fellow cheapskates on the subject: You can maybe, perhaps, live sort-of comfortably on Social Security alone IF:

1. **You retire entirely debt-free, including owning a mortgage-free home or having no other cost for housing.** Once again, from the cheapskate's perspective, the biggest asset you can have going into retirement is NO DEBT and a minimal dependency on cash flow for your continued comfort and happiness. Particularly, having no housing costs (i.e., either your home is fully paid for, or you're living rent-free with a family member, for example) is obviously a real game-changer when you look at the prospect of surviving on Social Security alone. "Not having a mortgage or other housing costs is really the big thing," Jean Setzfand says about the prospects for getting by on Social Security benefits alone, a proposition that she views as extremely difficult but unfortunately increasingly common.

2. **You retire in good health.** Of course, even if you are fortunate enough to be in good health going into retirement, there's no guarantee as to whether your health will continue to hold up. Nonetheless, at least having a modicum of good health when you enter retirement—and working like heck to maintain and even improve it as much as possible (see Chapter 7)—is not only critical to minimizing out-of-pocket health-care expenses, it's also essential in terms of maintaining the option of reentering the workforce if you need additional income.

3. **You are entitled to Social Security benefits at or close to the maximum retirement benefits possible.** The level of benefits you receive under Social Security depends on two things: the age you choose to start drawing benefits, and the duration and level at which you paid into Social Security during your working years. The range of benefits individuals receive under the system can be dramatically different, at least in terms of relative comparisons. For example, someone retiring in 2011 at the age of sixty-six could receive a monthly benefit of $2,366 if they earned the maximum taxable amount every year from age twenty-one onward. That's slightly more than DOUBLE the average monthly benefit paid out in 2011 ($1,177), a difference that could make *all the difference* in covering at least your truly essential expenses during retirement. In fact, if you and your spouse (or housemate) both receive monthly Social Security benefits of,

say, $2,050, your annual income would be on a par with the median annual income of all American households in 2010 ($49,445). At that level—particularly if you retire debt- and mortgage-free and in relatively good health— living a fairly comfortable life on Social Security alone should not be terribly difficult.

What is the best age at which to start drawing Social Security benefits? While there are many individual variables to factor in, the conventional wisdom is that it generally pays to postpone collecting Social Security as long as possible . . . unless you have reason to believe that you're going to die relatively young. Because monthly benefit amounts increase significantly the longer you hold off on collecting, if you're healthy and can afford it, studies show that in the end you're likely to come out ahead (in total lifetime payout) by waiting. For example, if you can claim benefits at age sixty-two (currently the earliest age you can claim benefits) at, say, $1,000 per month, that will increase to about $1,333 per month if you wait until you're sixty-six (full retirement age) and to roughly $1,750 per month if you wait until age seventy to collect benefits. That's a whopping 75 percent increase in monthly benefits—payable for the rest of your life—for waiting the additional eight years. By the way, as stated in Cheapskate Retirement Principle #9, that same general rule—wait as long as you can afford to wait before drawing (without incurring any penalties)—applies not just to Social Security but to other funds you have stashed away for retirement, since most people don't know how long they're going to live.

4. **You have a spouse or housemate who is also entitled to a healthy level of Social Security benefits.** As discussed in the next chapter, marriage—or even shacking up or living platonically with a housemate—has many financial benefits, particularly in retirement. Since Social Security is currently designed to replace 30 to 40 percent of most people's preretirement income, a household with two retirees receiving benefits could perhaps replace 60 to 80 percent of at least one of the recipients' preretirement incomes, which for a couple of cohabiting cheapskates could go a long ways. Of course, as we've seen before, basing your retirement income needs on your preretirement income can be grossly misleading, so when you crunch your real expense numbers, the gap between your actual expenses and the monthly Social Security benefits of a household with two benefit-earners may not be as big as you think.

Keep in mind, though, that when one spouse dies, the surviving spouse is normally entitled to continue to receive the larger of the two benefits, but not both. To help mitigate what could be a significant drop in household income in the event of one spouse's death, married couples often choose to maximize the highest-earning spouse's benefit by having that person delay collecting Social Security until age seventy. That way, whichever spouse lives longest has the option of continuing that larger benefit. In essence, this move serves almost like a type of life insurance for the surviving spouse, estimated by some financial planners to be the equivalent of $50,000 to $250,000 of a life insurance benefit.

5. **You live in a state that doesn't tax Social Security benefits.** Currently thirty-six states do not tax Social Security benefits. The other fourteen states tax benefits to varying extents, with a number taxing benefits to the same or similar extent as they are taxed on your federal tax returns. Under federal tax law, you pay federal taxes on Social Security benefits if you file a return as an individual and your total income is more the $25,000, or if you file a joint return and you and your spouse have a total income of more than $32,000. A listing of the states that do not tax Social Security benefits—along with a very useful summary of retirement-related tax issues for each of the fifty states—can be found on the Kiplinger website at www.kiplinger.com/tools/retiree_map/index .html?map=6#anchor.

6. **You have other savings or some other security net to fall back on in case of an emergency.** For most people, implicit in the phrase "comfortable retirement" is having the peace of mind of knowing that if some emergency comes up, you have the financial or other resources

available to help weather the storm. Even if you are able to cover your routine expenses with Social Security alone, you're likely to be left with little, if anything, extra to cover even the smallest unexpected expense. Obviously, the best source of security and peace of mind is an ample, diversified, accessible selection of investments and other savings instruments. But if you already have that, then you're probably not choosing to live on Social Security alone, unless your Social Security Stretcher's Syndrome is particularly acute. Tapping the equity in your home (see Chapter 6), selling off items of value, and various forms of insurance—or even the knowledge that you can depend on the support of willing family members or friends in a worst-case scenario—could serve as at least a partial substitute for a traditional financial safety net of investments and other savings.

7. **You live in a locale with a low cost of living, including property and other taxes.** Call me a nerd, but I love pouring over the Cost of Living Index (COLI) and Consumer Price Index (CPI), both available through the Bureau of Labor Statistics website (www.bls.gov). These are the indices that monitor and compare the prices of goods and services over time in various places around the country. The COLI is based on a compilation of data from several sources related to the cost of housing, food, utilities, health, transportation, and miscellaneous.

The index is constructed so that the nationwide average equals 100 and the cost of living in each of the 140 or so urban areas included in the COLI is read as a percentage in comparison to the national average. So, in the 2010 COLI, for example, Rochester, New York, just happened to have an index of exactly 100.00 percent, meaning its cost of living is precisely on a par with the national average cost of living. In the same year, New York City/Manhattan had the highest cost of living at 216.7 percent ("Holy Big Apple, Batman!")—more than twice the national average—while Harlingen, Texas, north of Brownsville, had the lowest cost of living at 82.8 percent, or about 17 percent less than the national average. Since your Social Security benefit remains the same no matter where you live (although taxes on benefits vary by state), you might be able to stretch the spending power of your benefit dollars by 10 to 20 percent or even more by relocating to a locale with a lower cost of living. It's also important to note that the COLI does not reflect the cost of state and local taxes in the different urban areas it examines; one of the best online resources for comparing state and local taxes in locations across the country can be found at www.bankrate.com/finance/taxes/check-taxes-in-your-state.aspx.

8. **You have a reasonable ability to earn additional income if needed.** Like Rob Harden, it's understandable if in

retirement you prefer a tackle box to a toolbox when it comes to how you spend your free time. But Harden is doing the smart thing by keeping his options open regarding the possibility of needing—or even *wanting*—to go back to work part-time to supplement his Social Security benefits. Of course, that requires having both the physical and the mental capacities to reenter the workforce, as well as the skills and network to find appropriate employment. But since you can currently earn $14,640 a year without losing any Social Security benefits if you're a beneficiary under full retirement age—and $38,880 a year without any loss of benefits when you reach full retirement age—at least having the option of working part-time in retirement provides significant peace of mind, since it could more than double the monthly income the average retiree receives from Social Security alone without any decrease in benefits. Plus, as we'll see in Chapter 8, earning some extra income during retirement to augment your Social Security benefits may even be more enjoyable than it is financially rewarding.

So with all that said, relying solely on Social Security for a *comfortable enough* retirement shouldn't be entirely dismissed as a cheapskate fantasy, even though neither I, nor any other financial pundit I know, would recommend it as prudent retirement planning. And as a practical matter, you need to understand and appreciate the big old qualifier I put on my earlier claim: "Maybe, but probably *only if you can really afford not to.*"

☞ *You might need a Cheapskate Intervention if you declare your houseplants as dependents on your tax returns.*

By that I mean that if you take a look at a number of the preconditions on the above list—a fully paid-off mortgage, zero debt, a safety net to fall back on, maximum Social Security benefits, and so on—you realize that in order to get to those enviable positions, chances are you've had a career that has left you with considerably more retirement assets than Social Security alone.

If nothing else, in order to qualify for the maximum Social Security retirement benefit possible, you must have paid into the system at the maximum taxable amount every year during your career. That means that you'd currently be earning at least $110,100 a year if you're still working. I doubt that few people earning that kind of money aren't finding the wherewithal to sock at least some of it away for retirement or other savings . . . but then again, some people's ability to squander money never ceases to surprise me.

Rob Harden agrees. "Hell, if you're earning that kind of income while you're still working (i.e., the maximum amount subject to Social Security withholding), then you're not going to be leading a lifestyle that can be supported by

Social Security alone, even if you do receive the maximum benefit amount. Let's face it, Jeff, if you're earning that kind of money, you're probably looking at your Social Security check as something that *might* cover your country club fees once you're retired, if you're lucky."

Cheapskate Retirement Principle #9

With Social Security—as well as other sources of retirement income—the longer you can afford to postpone drawing on it (without incurring any penalties), the better, unless you have a crystal ball and know exactly how long you're going to live. By waiting an additional eight years (age seventy versus age sixty-two) to draw Social Security, for example, your monthly benefit will be about 75 percent greater . . . and that's for the rest of your life.

FOR MORE INFORMATION ON SOCIAL SECURITY AND YOUR POSSIBLE BENEFITS

Fully understanding the Social Security system and how to maximize the benefits you may be entitled to can be complex. But it's well worth spending the time to research exactly how Social Security may affect you and your specific retirement situation. Here are some terrific online resources to help you learn more:

- **US Social Security Administration** (www.ssa.gov): A very robust, user-friendly website, with a number of particularly helpful features:
  - ► **www.ssa.gov/retire2:** Square one when it comes to exploring the wealth of retirement planning information available on the SSA site and getting your questions answered.
  - ► **www.ssa.gov/estimator:** A free calculator tool that allows you to enter a few personal facts and your Social Security number and then calculates monthly benefits based on different retirement ages—probably the best five minutes you can spend when it comes to retirement planning.
  - ► **www.socialsecurity.gov/applyonline:** And when you're ready to apply for Social Security benefits, go here to apply online.

- **AARP** (www.AARP.org): AARP has an enhanced Social Security benefits calculator of its own (www.aarp.org /SocialSecurityBenefits). It's a sort of tricked-out version of the calculator on the SSA site, allowing you to add in some personalized expense information to give you an estimate of how much of your living expenses will be covered by Social Security based on various assumptions.

JERRY DYSON

Happiness Is Wanting What You Have

"I've learned how to be poor and very happy." Jerry Dyson wrote those words about himself for a presentation he gave a few years ago, and as I drove home from interviewing him at his modest apartment in the Columbia Heights neighborhood of northwest Washington, DC, I kept asking myself: *Is Jerry Dyson really a poor man?*

Statistically, the seventy-seven-year-old isn't living below the official poverty line set by the US Department of Health and Human Services. For a single person like Jerry living in Washington, DC, you would need an income of $10,890 or less to be considered "poor" by those standards (per 2011 statistics). Fortunately, Dyson receives more than that in Social Security benefits alone, plus he has a small pension from when he worked at the *Washington Post*. He also generates some additional income from a host of little side businesses he "plays around with," including professional photography, PR consulting, and selling customized cards and invitations, an enterprise that he started at the age of fourteen and has maintained ever since. He estimates that he spends roughly $1,500 per month on all of his living expenses, including what he pays for his quasi-rent-controlled apartment.

Official poverty-level gauges aside, it's clear that Jerry is among that half of all Americans who rely primarily on Social Security for their retirement income. Without it, he would be "poor" by any and every definition of the term. But what's indisputable is the second half of Jerry Dyson's statement: "I've learned how to be poor *and very happy*."

"Sure, I could have more stuff and could afford to spend at least a little more than I do. But all it would do is create more pains in the ass. Like, if I had a car here, I'd have to pay to park it, and insure it, and check on it all the time. You don't own things, things own you," he says of the relatively spartan lifestyle he lives, partly out of necessity and partly out of choice. Hearing Jerry talk, a favorite saying comes to mind: "The happiest people don't have the best of everything; they just make the best of everything they have."

Looking around his two-room apartment, which I would estimate to be not much more than three hundred square feet total, it's clear that Jerry does indeed make the best of everything he has. I'm reminded a little of being in a ship captain's quarters, where every inch of space is cleverly utilized, neatly organized, and attractively decorated in a water-related motif.

The apartment building and the apartments themselves have definitely seen better days. The neighborhood is currently enjoying some revitalization, but it's still pretty sketchy. On one side of Georgia Avenue, you have the nicely maintained campus of Howard University, filled with bright young students from around the world. And on the other side are liquor stores, occasional abandoned buildings, and an old man sleeping on the sidewalk during the middle of the day, a half-empty quart of King Cobra malt liquor by his side.

But Jerry has made his own compact space very comfortable and has designed it for maximum efficiency. A small sitting area with two chairs, the walls lined with fabric ("to reduce noise") and covered with family photos and other memorabilia. A good-size desk and credenza—fashioned in large part from scrap lumber, including an old door—and floor-to-ceiling bookshelves filled with meticulously labeled notebooks, the nerve center of Jerry's various selfish employment ventures. A simple galley-style kitchen, a truly tiny room with two built-in bunk beds exactly like in a Pullman car, and a basic bathroom with 1950-era fixtures.

"On my fifty-seventh birthday I went to lunch from my job at the *Washington Post*, and you might say I've been on lunch break ever since," Jerry tells me, recalling the day he officially retired after spending twenty-eight years working as a graphic artist at the newspaper. Jerry has rented this apartment for many years, even during a time when he also had a house in the DC suburbs. "Since the rent was so low and I was working night shifts and odd hours, it was convenient to have a place close by to stay sometimes, rather than go all the way out to the house. When I retired from the *Post*, I decided to downsize my life big-time and move in here permanently, although I do spend a lot of time back home in Louisiana."

Born and raised in the tiny town of Franklinton, Louisiana, Jerry and his four brothers and one sister grew up in a home he still owns today with his surviving siblings. His father was a barber and a builder, his mother a part-time beautician and full-time homemaker. Young Jerry shined shoes for customers in his dad's barber shop. Jerry recalls that the Dysons' house was "kind of like a community center for all the Black kids in town. . . . We had space for playing baseball, volleyball, basketball, boxing, all kinds of sports."

Forgetting his age, I naively asked, "Was the town primarily Black? You said it was like a community center for Black kids?"

"No. You need to remember, Jeff, this was back when down South there was a *dual system*," he says, drawing out his pronunciation of the final two words just a little for what

I interpret as a bit of subtle satire. "Whites had their facilities and Blacks had to have their own. So our house functioned as sort of the unofficial community center for Black kids, although anyone was welcome to join in."

Despite the fact that neither of Jerry's parents had attended college, the senior Dysons placed a priority on their children's education. Five of their six children attended college, with his parents managing to come up with the money for tuition, although Jerry's various self-employment ventures helped supplement his college fund. Jerry graduated from Southern University, Baton Rouge, in 1957 with a degree in art education, and—after serving three years in the army as a photographer and a couple of years teaching high school back in Louisiana—he eventually ended up in DC and went on to complete the course work for a master's degree in communication at American University. He had served temporary duty in DC during his time in the army and decided to relocate there because "I wanted to live someplace for a change where they didn't sleep at night, if you know what I mean." He shows me a photo of himself during that period, and I immediately have a flash image of a young, good-looking Denzel Washington.

After his ("one and only!") marriage ended in the mid-seventies, Jerry supplemented his income from the *Washington Post* by usually holding down at least one other part-time job at the same time in order to afford the $600 per month in child support he paid for the couple's only child, their daughter Jeri. Much of his side work involved sales, something he readily admits has been a lifelong passion. "Over the years, I've sold everything from automobiles, books, detergent, fruit, graphics, insurance, newspapers, pots and pans, trucks, vegetables, and even zebra skins for a while," he says with a rich, deep laugh.

Chief among Jerry's advice for living happily on a small retirement income is to "plan, get organized, and stay that way," he says, while making probably the fifth trip across the room that morning to pluck another notebook off the bookshelves to show me. This one contains a variety of budgeting and scheduling worksheets he's developed over the years to keep his financial affairs on track and manage his time wisely.

He's also a big believer in remaining selfishly employed during retirement—both to augment his income and fill his time—and says he has no plans to ever curtail his custom-printed card business or his other little enterprises, although he does plan to eventually turn them over to younger family members. He may also at some point decide to move back to his boyhood home in Louisiana permanently, where he says he could "live like a prince" on what he spends living in DC, and where he could hunt, fish, and raise a garden. I guess after nearly fifty years in the big city, the idea of returning to a place where people do indeed sleep at night is gaining some appeal. And he's also finding plenty of time at this point in his life to be involved in a host of community service and fraternal organizations, including his church and his old army unit's 97th Signal Battalion

Association (www.triedandtrue.org), which sponsors various kinds of charitable work.

When Jerry talks about his daughter, now forty-one, you can see the pride written all across his marbled face. In the tradition set by his parents, placing a priority on education, Jerry made a significant sacrifice of his own by drawing down and eventually depleting the 401(k) account he'd established while working at the *Washington Post* in order to help fund his daughter's college education, including medical school.

"Yes, sir," he says, sitting up a little straighter in his chair as he speaks, "today my daughter Jeri is a pediatrician at the Bethesda Naval Hospital, and that's something that makes me very, very proud. When we were talking earlier about what makes someone happy, what's important in life, that's my answer . . . that's what's important to me. It's not about getting things you don't have, it's about giving thanks every day for what you do have."

Reflecting on those words, by the time I turn into our driveway after my interview with Jerry, I realize that Jerry Dyson may be many things, but what he clearly *isn't* is a poor man.

CHAPTER 6

Simple-Size *Your Way to a* *Better Retirement*

"Simplify, simplify, simplify! I say, let your affairs be as two or three, and not a hundred or a thousand; instead of a million count half a dozen, and keep your accounts on your thumb-nail."

The quote is from Henry David Thoreau, but it's Bob Johnson who is reciting it to me from memory as the two of us barrel down the Pennsylvania Turnpike, headed to Pittsburgh for a regional meeting of the American Youth Hostels. By that time, I'd known Bob for more than five years, and I'd grown to respect and admire him in many ways. Including his ability to extemporaneously recite passages of philosophy and scripture like the one he'd just rattled off so casually.

Bob had a degree in theology but never formally practiced in the clergy. So I always imagined he had a natural gift for memorizing such profound bits of wisdom. Whereas in my case, if it isn't an off-color limerick that starts with the words "There once was a man from Nantucket . . . ," I immediately get tongue-tied.

"It's really true, you know," Bob said. "Whenever you have two options, one simple and the other more complex, I've generally found the simplest path to be the best choice." We'd been having another wide-ranging conversation about life—including money—and the point he was making applied to both.

"How so?" I asked.

"Well, Mr. Ton-tog-an-y . . . is that how you pronounce it? The simplest choices are usually the most cost-effective. But here's the best thing of all: I've also found they tend to involve less stress and make you happier in the long run. Never underestimate the value of simplicity. Capiche?" Bob concluded as he eased back a little on the gas pedal when he spotted a Pennsylvania Highway Patrol car lying in wait up ahead.

"Yah, I guess so, and I think I actually agree with you on this one," I said. "After all, 'Ton-tog-an-y' is Algonquin for 'Keep it simple, stupid.' Didn't you know that, Bob?" I added, beating him to the inevitable punch.

Taking Stock of Your Life . . . and Your Stuff

While simplifying your life as much as possible and as early as possible can dramatically increase your financial security leading up to retirement, it's never too late to *simple-size*, as I call it. Simple-sizing is like "downsizing," but, as Bob pointed out to me that day, it's grounded in an understanding that whenever you choose the simplest path, it generally saves you the most money, generates less stress, and results in greater happiness. Particularly as you prepare for and enter retirement, it pays to place a premium on achieving all three of those ends.

Of course, the place to start when it comes to simple-sizing is with the big stuff, including housing, transportation, communications, and all of the excess baggage you've likely amassed over the years. And when it comes to excess baggage, why not include a review of the emotional and personal luggage you're carrying around with you as well as part of your exercise in simple-sizing? That'll definitely produce less stress and make you happier.

This is the time to step back from your current life, and ask yourself some important questions, including:

- Do I really still need or want this [fill in the blank]? (Assuming you ever really needed or wanted it in the first place!)
- When was the last time I actually used or appreciated this _____?
- What would my life be like if I woke up tomorrow morning and this _____ was no longer something I owned? What's the worst that could happen? What's the best that could happen?
- Do I know of someone who would appreciate and benefit from owning/using this_____ more than I do?

- Is this _____ worth selling or trading for something else (including money) that is of more value to me at this point in my life?
- How much is it costing me to continue to own this

  _____

  (e.g., to maintain it, to insure it, to store it, etc.)?
- Given the remote possibility that I might not live forever, what's likely to happen to this _____ after I'm gone? Will it be kept and valued by someone I know, or will it be sold or thrown away? Will it be more of a blessing or more of a burden to someone if I still own this on the day I depart for the big Dollar Store in the sky?

Given that the average US household is likely to contain literally tens of thousands of individual items (assuming you count every last paper clip), getting a handle on what you already own and evaluating whether or not it makes sense to get rid of some of it can be a time-consuming and even an overwhelming process.

Difficulty aside, putting together a basic household inventory is the place to start. Taking the time—and it will no doubt take some time—to catalogue at least the major, most valuable things you own will accomplish three things: (1) It's important for insurance purposes, as a record should your valuables be stolen or damaged, or should you realize that you are under- or overinsured. (2) It will give you (and your heirs) some ready estimates of the value of your individual possessions should you find yourself in a situation where you need to sell some of them to generate extra cash. (3) It's likely to be a screaming wake-up call, reminding you just how much stuff you probably own and what a small percentage of it you actually ever use.

In that last instance, preparing a household inventory is like foreplay leading up to the actual decluttering process. When you put it like that, creating a household inventory sounds rather titillating, doesn't it?

The good news is there are a number of online resources to help make pulling together a household inventory easier, less time-consuming, and even kind of fun. For starters, the website for the Federal Emergency Management Agency (www.FEMA.org) provides advice on what types of items you should inventory and how to document them. The Insurance Information Institute's website, www.knowyourstuff.org, offers a free program with software that allows you to sort and inventory items by each room in your house, recording values, pictures, serial/model numbers, and so forth. Many insurance companies offer their own guidelines and inventory spreadsheets to their customers, and you can find information on a range of free downloadable home inventory spreadsheets and software on the following two websites:

PCWorld: www.pcworld.com/article/236650/download_a_free_homeinventory_spreadsheet.html

Squawkfox: www.squawkfox.com/2008/10/24/15-free
-printable-home-inventory-worksheets

Cheapskate Retirement Principle #10

Simple-sizing is like downsizing, but it's based on recognizing that whenever you simplify your life, it usually saves you money, and also reduces your stress and makes you happier. Particularly before you retire, the rule is "Lose it if you don't use it."

Should You Relocate When You Retire and/or Downsize Your Home?

We've seen numerous examples in this book of how cheapskates have, for the most part, made very smart choices throughout their lives when it comes to housing, and how those choices are one of the most important factors in allowing them to retire better, earlier, and happier. Specifically:

- They tend to buy a less expensive home than they can afford, at least according to industry lending standards, as the newlyweds Kelly and Jon Nowak are in the process of doing.
- They tend to stay in that home for a relatively long pe-

riod of time compared to typical American homeowners, often buying a "forever home" as the first—and only—home they'll ever buy.

- They tend to pay off their home mortgages earlier than required, like Shelle and Jonathan Cedotal in Jackson, Mississippi.

- They often buy a home that has the potential to generate income for them (e.g., a duplex or a home with other rental unit possibilities), like Denise and I have done.

- And they sometimes even partner with other people to jointly buy a home, as Lys and Dan Burden did with the first home they owned.

Since housing—regardless of whether you rent or buy—is for most people their single largest lifetime expense, it pays to seriously consider these precepts for cheapskate homeownership before you ever go shopping for your very first home. If you do, it's a game-changer not just in your everyday financial life and outlook, but particularly as you plan for and enter retirement.

☞ *You might need a Cheapskate Intervention if you watch QVC 24/7, except when* Hoarders *is on, because it gives you good ideas for how to organize all your stuff.*

But what if it's too late for all of that? What if you're already in a home that has few or none of the features mentioned above? What if it's a bigger home than you need or than you can afford, or not a place where you want to spend what's left of your *forever*? Should you sell your home and relocate, or find some other way to simple-size your housing situation?

The answers to those questions are anything but simple, since so many different variables may apply, but here are a few options and principles to seriously consider:

1. **Remember Cheapskate Retirement Principle #2:** You know, the one discussed in Chapter 2 about paying off all personal debt before you retire, *including* your home mortgage. Cheapskates feel so strongly about that principle, we say that until you're debt-free, you are—by definition—*not* ready to retire. In order to pay off your home mortgage (as well as other debts), delaying retirement and/or selling off other assets are options, but selling your current home and using the equity to fully pay for a new, less expensive home might also be a possibility. Of course, it all depends on how much you still owe on your current home, how easily it can be sold, the tax implications of selling it, and if you have enough equity to buy someplace else that sufficiently meets your needs. Nonetheless, it's an option to consider, as is selling your home and moving into an affordable apartment, like Jerry Dyson did when he retired.

2. **Never Underestimate the Savings from Living in a Smaller Space:** Assuming that you do decide to relocate

when you retire—in order to retire debt-free or for other financial/lifestyle reasons—carefully calculate all of the savings you're likely to incur by moving into a space smaller than the one you might currently inhabit. This was also something my friend Bob Johnson always talked a lot about: "When most people go shopping for a home, they want as much space as they can possibly afford. The only question they ask themselves is, 'Can we afford the mortgage payments on that house that is four hundred square feet larger than the other house we just looked at?' But, once again, they're not seeing the total true costs. They don't think about how much owning those extra four hundred square feet is going to cost them every day, going forward . . . to insure it, to heat it, to cool it, to pay taxes on it, to repair and maintain it, even to decorate it. And, of course, to pay that much more interest on an even larger mortgage, all for some extra space they may very well decide they really don't need or rarely use." When it comes to living comfortably in a smaller space, check out the *Not So Big House* series of books by Sarah Susanka and the website www .ApartmentTherapy.com for some terrific tips and ideas.

3. **Consider a One-Hour-or-Less Move:** "But we love where we're living, because it's so close to all of our friends and family." This is something you hear a lot when people consider relocating in their retirement. And it's a valid point for many people. But "relocating" doesn't need to always

involve moving hundreds or thousands of miles from where you currently call home. "I crunched the numbers, and I decided we could afford to retire five years earlier than we planned if we just moved to *the wrong side of the tracks*," cheapskate Benny Paul told me. A longtime resident of the Minneapolis metro area, he and his wife, Betty, had raised their three daughters in their home in one of the city's nicest suburbs, moving there in part because of the excellent public schools that their daughters attended. After they became empty nesters, the house was more space than they needed—or wanted—and so the Pauls started thinking about relocating. "We debated about moving to Florida after I retired," Benny says, "but our kids and grandkids and all our friends are in this area. So then we started thinking about just staying where we were or maybe trying to find something a little smaller in the same neighborhood." Even though Benny's planned retirement was still a few years away, the Pauls started doing a little preliminary research into what was on the market in their neighborhood. Then their search gradually expanded outward, but: "We agreed that we wouldn't consider moving anyplace farther than an hour away from where we currently live," Benny says. "We couldn't believe what we could afford to buy in the next county over. Years ago it wasn't considered a very decent place to live . . . a little seedy, to put it mildly," Betty says of the other neighborhoods they began researching, "in part because the homes were smaller and older and the schools weren't very good. But now it's a safe and respectable area, and schools are no longer important to us. Plus we're specifically looking for a smaller house." The Pauls found that they could sell their current home, move to "the other side of the tracks," and walk away with enough surplus cash that Benny could retire years earlier than planned.* "To have that many more years to enjoy our retirement together and spend time with our family, we'll gladly drive a few extra miles," Betty says.

4. **Or Consider Moving Halfway Across the Country, or Halfway Around the World:** If you don't have family or friends or any other reason to remain rooted to your current locale, it truly is possible—and exciting—to retire to another part of the country or even to another country entirely, where you can live extremely comfortably on relatively little money compared to many places in the United States. In Chapter 5, I discussed the Cost of Living Index and tax implications pertaining to Social Security benefits when it comes to the possibility of relocating in retirement. But in terms of other financial and lifestyle considerations (e.g., climate, health care, safety services, recreational opportunities, etc.), here are some invaluable resources to consult if you're looking to make a major move when you retire:

---

* Be sure to consult a tax specialist regarding the tax implications of selling your home in order to relocate in retirement.

- **www.BestPlaces.net** The Sperling's BestPlaces website is a gold mine of information, allowing you to compare thousands of US metro areas, cities, and even neighborhoods against one another in almost every conceivable way—from crime rates and cost of living, to the least/most stressful places, to even the "manliest cities in America" (funny, Tontogany didn't make that list). The site is free (they do encourage you to register for a free membership, and since it truly is "free," why not?), and it's the kind of place where you'll likely spend hours digging into the endless data and getting a glimpse into what your life could be like if you moved hither and yon.

- **www.retirementliving.com** This is the website of the Retirement Living Information Center and provides information on a range of retirement-related issues, in addition to comparison data if you're considering relocating to another part of the country (including planned retirement communities and senior housing facilities). Some information on the site is accessible free of charge, although a one-time membership of $24.95 gets you unlimited access for life.

- **www.aarp.org/home-garden/livable-communities /location-scout-find-best-place-live** The "Location Scout" tool on the AARP website is a quick and fun little exercise. Answer a series of online questions (taking less than ten minutes to complete) about everything from preferred climate and cost of living to the importance you place on having access to all kinds of things, like public libraries and professional sports teams, and then the "Location Scout" spits out a selection of US locales that might be a good match for you.

- And if you're looking for possible retirement spots outside of the United States, some favorite resources include: www.escapefromamerica.com; www.expatforum .com; www.escapeartist.com; and the indispensable book *How to Retire Overseas: Everything You Need to Know to Live Well (for Less) Abroad,* by Kathleen Peddicord.

One word of caution, though, about the seemingly endless stream of "best places to retire" lists that you see all the time: once a specific city or town has made "the list," chances are it's probably well into its renaissance as a retirement hotspot, so it's likely to be less affordable and attractive in other ways than it was before the spotlight hit it. Nonetheless, these lists can be useful as general guides in determining areas of the country (or the world) that you might want to consider and research more closely.

☞ *You might need a Cheapskate Intervention if you own a snowmobile and live in Florida.*

5. Instead of Downsizing, Add More People: If you love the home you're in, but it's more space than you really need and maybe more costly than you can afford, consider staying put and just bringing in more people. If zoning laws and codes allow, think about retrofitting your home—like the Burdens are doing—to convert extra space into a rental unit . . . and extra income. Or invite a friend, relative, or (better yet) a new lover to move in and help share expenses and provide companionship. Brothers Hank and Bobby McLean of Omaha, Nebraska, had grown apart over the years, but after both of their wives passed away within a year of each other, the brothers patched up some old differences and rediscovered the camaraderie they'd enjoyed in their younger years. Eventually they realized that Bobby's big old clapboard house was plenty roomy enough for the two of them, so Hank sold his house and moved in with Bobby. "For the most part, it's nice having the company, and living together lets us stretch our Social Security checks a good bit further," Bobby says, adding with a wink, "even though Hank can be a real pain in the patootie sometimes."

6. **A Word About Reverse Mortgages:** Rather than selling their current home and moving to someplace less expensive and perhaps augmenting their retirement nest egg in the process (like Benny and Betty Paul), an increasing number of people are staying put and turning to reverse mortgages instead. Reverse mortgages are a special type of loan that allows you to borrow against the equity you have in your home and use the

proceeds of the loan for whatever purposes you choose. Unlike a traditional home equity loan, with a reverse mortgage, the loan doesn't need to be paid back starting immediately; it is repaid when you die, move, or sell your home, or if you default on the loan by not paying property taxes or homeowner's insurance or by failing to maintain the property appropriately. To qualify for a reverse mortgage, you must be at least sixty-two years old and own your home outright or be able to pay off your home with the proceeds from the reverse mortgage. You should also know that reverse mortgages are notoriously complicated and involve significant upfront fees. See the website of the US Department of Housing and Urban Development for a comprehensive explanation of reverse mortgages and related regulations: http://portal.hud.gov /hudportal/HUD?src=/program_offices/housing/sfh /hecm.

So are reverse mortgages a good idea for people looking to retire better, earlier, and happier? The prevailing cheapskate wisdom on the topic is that, at best, they should be considered a "source of last resort" for most people. If for no other reason than the hefty upfront fees, it's usually best to explore all other options for reducing expenses and tap other available assets before resorting to a reverse mortgage. And, if you do, in keeping with Cheapskate Retirement Principle #11, the longer you can wait in life before tapping the equity in your home through a reverse mortgage or other instrument (e.g., a traditional home equity loan or refinancing), the better.

7. **Consider the Cost of Transportation Carefully:** Next to housing and health care, the single largest expense for most retirees is transportation; in fact, on average, it's virtually tied with health care as the second-biggest expense for retirees. As we saw in the profile of Lys and Dan Burden, one of the primary reasons they chose the retirement location they did was that it will allow them to live car-free or at least "car-lite," saving them an estimated $11,500 per year. Whether or not you're relocating in retirement, thinking through your options when it comes to transportation is an extremely high priority. Can you downsize from owning two cars to just one? Can you live without a car completely—or at least keep it parked in the garage more often—by relying on public transportation, community-provided transportation for seniors, or car/ride-sharing programs? An excellent book on the topic about how to live car-free or car-lite is, ironically, entitled *How to Live Well Without Owning a Car*, by Chris Balish. Don't be put off by the title; in reality, Balish explores all types of creative options to simply reduce your automotive dependency (and costs), even if you decide to hang on to your four wheels once you retire.

Cheapskate Retirement Principle #11

Your house should probably be the "source of last resort" in terms of tapping it for cash through a reverse mortgage. But that doesn't mean it can't be an income producer (e.g., by renting out a portion of it or finding a roommate) or that you can't reduce your cost of living and perhaps increase your nest egg by relocating to a less expensive area or home.

"I Never Knew I Could Afford to Retire Until I Cleaned Out the Barn"

To inspire you in your efforts to simple-size and declutter your life, consider the following cheapskate testimonial.

Marv Johnson is a pack rat, and he'll make no attempt to deny it. His late wife, Joan, shared his passion for frequenting yard sales, flea markets, and—best of all—farm and estate auctions, which are still commonplace in northern Indiana, where the couple spent their entire forty-two years of married life.

"We never had a lot of money, and we never spent much of it at auctions or sales, either. It was just something fun to do . . . something to do together," Marv says. For the Johnsons, occasional trips to the granddaddy of all midwestern flea markets, the one held during the summer months in

Shipshewana, Indiana, were like pilgrimages to Mecca. "Man, oh man, until you've seen Shipshewana in full swing, you just can't imagine it.

"It sounds crazy, Jeff, but a lot of times we'd just buy boxes full of junk, mostly at auctions, without even knowing what was in them. All we knew was that we had three or four dollars between the two of us to spend that day, so if a box was going for a quarter or fifty cents, *that* was a box for us."

Because the Johnsons lived on a farmette with a good-sized barn, Marv says they got into the habit of just briefly rummaging through the boxes a little bit when they got them home and then packing them away in the barn with the intention of examining them more closely in the future. "The exciting part for us was bidding on the stuff and getting a great price. Guess we sort of lost interest once we got home . . . all that haggling can tire you out, you know."

When Joan suddenly passed away while attending a church event a few years ago, Marv was devastated. "I'd not only lost my wife, I'd lost my best friend," he tells me, with his eyes welling up. "I don't mind telling you I was so depressed, to the point of thinking seriously about making a date with the barrel of my shotgun."

Still working partial shifts at a nearby RV manufacturing plant, Marv had just turned sixty-one and was looking at a pretty skimpy Social Security check as his sole means of support in retirement. He still owed a small amount on the couple's home and even more on a new pickup truck he'd bought before Joan's death. Understandably, Marv's dismal retirement prospects darkened his mood all the more.

"One day I was so low I couldn't get any lower, and I went out to that barn, not knowing what I was going to do next. I just starting kicking the shit out of those boxes of stuff Joan and I had bought over the years . . . feeling sorry for myself and mad at the world," he says. Eventually Marv got hold of his emotions and decided cleaning out the barn would give him something to do and keep his mind off his sorrows and troubles. Every evening after he got home from his shift, he'd head out to the barn to sort through more boxes, sometimes working until the wee hours of the following morning.

☞ *You might need a Cheapskate Intervention if you have an entire room in your house named after a sports team, a celebrity, or an activity you haven't participated in since college.*

"At first, I was unpacking boxes of stuff we'd only bought right before Joan passed away," Marv remembers. "None of it was interesting or worth very much . . . just junk." Nonetheless he began sorting it all out into five large wooden shipping crates he set up in the barn: one was stuff to throw away; another was for items to try to sell; the next contained things Marv could use himself; and the biggest crate was for things to give to friends or family or to donate to the thrift store his church operated. The fifth and final crate

Marv called the "Who Knows?" crate, reserved specifically for those items he just couldn't decide what to do with at the present time.

"Mostly, it was pretty easy to go through and sort it all out," he says, "because none of the stuff meant anything to Joan or me. What meant something was the memories of being together when we bought it . . . and I knew I'd always have those. I didn't need or want 99 percent of this stuff."

Marv was making steady progress every day in sorting through the more than forty years' worth of accumulated rummage, but in the process he realized two things. First, as he gradually worked his way toward the boxes closer to the back of the barn, their contents became more and more interesting, not to mention potentially valuable. "What I realized was that we'd bought boxes full of crap twenty, thirty, even forty years ago that wasn't worth squat at the time, but now some of it was antiques or at least collectibles." Some of the more valuable finds as Marv dug deeper into his barn-size time capsule: a massive collection of Matchbox cars (many in mint condition); dozens of highly collectible metal lunch boxes; vinyl record albums that had never been opened; dolls and other toys still in their original packaging; boxes filled with classic comic books, metal signs, and other vintage advertising memorabilia for everything from Tabasco sauce to Pepto-Bismol; and an entire box filled with nothing but PEZ dispensers.

The other thing Marv realized as he stood in the barn one evening staring at boxes still stacked all the way up as high as the hayloft, was that even at the rapid pace he was working, he might not live long enough to see the last box unpacked. So he enlisted the help of one of his daughters who lived nearby—"she knows all about selling stuff on eBay, is that what it's called?"—and with some muscle power supplied by his teenage grandsons, Team Marv really put their backs into the project.

By the time the project was complete more than nine months later, the barn was "empty as a pocket with a hole in it" (must be Indiana-speak), Marv's house and truck were paid for in full from the proceeds of all the items he'd sold, and he'd actually managed to set aside enough extra from the profits that he decided it was safe to retire at age sixty-five after all.

Plus Marv has two other new little income producers: he leases space in the now empty barn to people looking to store their boats and RVs, and he "saved back a few (dozen) boxes of the most special stuff" he and Joan bought over the years, so that Marv himself can now spend some enjoyable summer afternoons manning a sales table of his own at the Shipshewana flea market, making some other young couple's secondhand treasure hunting dreams come true.

LOSE IT IF YOU DON'T USE IT

"Not everybody has a barn full of stuff they can sell off," Marv Johnson openly admits, "but most people my age have a lot more things than they probably realize, and a lot of things they'd be better-off getting rid of."

With Marv and his army of PEZ dispensers as your inspiration, it pays in more ways than one to undertake a thorough decluttering exercise prior to retiring. Experts in decluttering and home organization generally give a thumbs-up to Marv's "five crates" approach, or some similar system of sorting items into categories, including: "Trash," "Save," "Sell," and "Giveaway." Many decluttering authorities even endorse Marv's creation of a "Who Knows?" category—a place to set some things aside at least temporarily rather than let the entire process get stymied while you agonize over what to do with a particular item. And creating individual "memory boxes"—collections of items associated with each of your children, for example—which you then pass along to them sooner rather than later, is also a commonly recommended decluttering technique.

Most experts in the field suggest working on decluttering a single room/space at a time, setting a schedule where you work a set number of hours per day/week at the process, and, with each item you see, asking yourself a simple question: *Do I love this and/or do I need this?* If you can't answer yes to either, then that item should NOT end up in the box marked "Save."

For more information on the art and science of de-cluttering, check out these helpful resources:

- ► 31 Days to Declutter Your Home: www.31daystodeclutter.com
- ► Life Organizers—Solutions for Organizing Your Life: www.lifeorganizers.com
- ► www.unclutter.com
- ► *The Joy of Less, a Minimalist Living Guide: How to Declutter, Organize, and Simplify Your Life,* by Francine Jay
- ► *The 100 Thing Challenge: How I Got Rid of Almost Everything, Remade My Life, and Regained My Soul,* by Dave Bruno
- ► And if you really have a problem overcoming clutter, consider contacting Clutterers Anonymous (http://sites.google.com/site/clutterersanonymous) or Hoarders Anonymous (www.hoardersanonymous .org).

BRUCE JACKSON

Live Simply So Others May Simply Live

"I never made much money, but it was always more than I needed."

It wasn't until the second time Bruce Jackson spoke those exact same words during my interview with him that the uniqueness of that simple statement fully registered in my brain.

"Bruce, how many people do you know who would ever say that?" I asked.

With a flash of his boyish smile and a sample of his

lilting little laugh that I found so engaging, Bruce replied: "Ha, ha . . . none that I know of! I told you I was peculiar. In fact, one of the things I noticed when I worked in the bank was that most people's expenses always rise to meet their income. When they'd come in to apply for yet another new loan, I'd notice that their income would almost always have increased since the last time they'd taken out a loan, but their expenses would have increased at least as much. So their assets hadn't increased at all, despite the fact that they were making more money."

Bruce also noticed that when people were delinquent on their bank loans, only about 10 percent of the time was the delinquency due to situations or emergencies truly out of their control. "Poor money management was nearly always the reason they were delinquent," he says, sadly shaking his head like a father who is disappointed in a child's irresponsible behavior.

At a youthful-appearing sixty-six, Jackson looks a little like a cross between Hugh Grant and a more distinguished version of Henry Winkler (aka "the Fonz"), if that's possible. He's clearly well read and a serious student of current affairs, and I'm sure that most people who see him around town in Lewisburg, Pennsylvania, assume that he's on the faculty of prestigious Bucknell University, which also calls Lewisburg home.

In reality, Bruce is largely a self-educated man, having attended college for a single year back in the 1960s before deciding that in his case the expense of a college education wasn't justified, given his ambivalence about future career plans. Instead, at the age of twenty, Bruce struck out on his own and settled down in Vermont, where he landed a clerking job with First Vermont Bank and eventually worked his way up to being a bank officer ("but they use that title very loosely in the banking world, so don't be overly impressed").

Looking at him today, you'd probably think Bruce was approaching retirement but maybe still had a couple of more years left in the career world. But the thing is, Jackson has been fully retired for more than twenty-five years, having retired at the age of thirty-nine. He's quick to point out, too, that for nine years prior to his full retirement, he was working only six months out of every year.

Bruce's secret for attaining financial independence so early in life had little to do with being a savvy investor, although he did buy a number of modest properties over the years in both Pennsylvania and Vermont, renting them out when he wasn't living in them and turning some over for decent but not spectacular profits. And his ability to retire at such a young age had even less to do with earning a big salary: the last year he worked at the bank (1985), he made $12,000, or about $25,000 in today's dollars.

No, the secret to Bruce's exceptionally early escape from the rat race is, in a nutshell, that he simply refused to allow his expenses to continually rise to meet his income. Sure, this allowed him to set aside some savings, most of which he has invested in low-risk, no-fee investments. "I may not have a lot of money, but since I already have more than I need, why would I risk losing it in higher-risk investments?" Bruce says. "Preservation of capital is the only important thing if you're already satisfied with what you have." And that's really the most valuable component of Bruce Jackson's formula for über-early retirement: finding your own "sweet spot"—the level at which you are satisfied with what you have—and not wasting your time or money chasing after more.

Bruce is the first person to admit that his relatively simple lifestyle is not for everyone. In fact, he seems to insist on prefacing every conversation with a statement to that effect, rattling it off like some sort of truth-in-lending disclosure statement from his days as a banker. "I lead a life that a lot of people would consider boring. I like predictability and a routine. I always have a good rapport with dogs," he says with another of his laughs and a sly grin. "You know, we both like routine. We're both easily pleased and satisfied."

But Bruce is as equally consistent in letting you know that while his life may appear boring to others, it's exactly the lifestyle he wants, and he doesn't consider it in any way a life of sacrifice, or hardship, or deprivations. "No one ever quite gets to utopia," he says with a slight philosophical pause, "but I have to stop and remind myself that, for me, I'm pretty close to it."

Bruce's days are filled with simple pleasures, most of which, as you might guess, are free. He makes full use of the many free or nominally priced programs and facilities offered by Bucknell University to the general public. In fact, when he was a bit younger and jogged every day, he made it a point to shower for the day in Bucknell's athletic facilities before returning home. That was one of the cost-saving measures that reduced his home water bill to the point where the utility company became suspicious, insisting that his water meter must be malfunctioning.

Jackson also enjoys walking and bicycling, adhering to a self-imposed "one-mile challenge," refusing to drive his car for any errand or other trip within a one-mile radius of his home, conditions permitting. What a smart and simple concept—for both staying fit and saving money—particularly since, according to a 2001 National Household Travel Survey, approximately 28 percent of all car trips made in the United States are to destinations within one mile of the starting point (and more than 40 percent are within two miles!).

"Yes, to other people I may seem boring, but I'm never bored," Bruce tells me in another self-deprecating moment. But I don't find Bruce or his simple lifestyle boring in the least. His eyes twinkle when he tells me about the tiny cabin (not quite two hundred square feet) he owns that sits on four wooded acres in Vermont—a place without electricity or running water ("but it does have a wood-fired outdoor bathtub!")—where he spends much of the summer. "It's a chance to really lead the simple life," he says of the time he spends at the cabin.

When in Lewisburg, Bruce lives with his longtime life partner, Carol, in an 1860s duplex they own jointly, and half of which they rent out. Although Bruce and Carol have been a couple for nearly twenty-five years, they've kept their finances separate (other than joint ownership of the duplex). "We decided that keeping our finances separate would eliminate a lot of potential problems, and it assures me that I'm carrying an equal share of the load despite my lesser income," Bruce explains.

As for Bruce's finances, he has an income of about $16,000 per year ($6,000 from interest and dividends; $2,500 from the duplex rental; and $7,500 from Social Security, which he began drawing at age sixty-two). Being entirely debt-free, Bruce says that he manages to live pretty much just on his Social Security benefits alone, with the exception of medical insurance and expenses, which force him to dip into his other income streams.

Although Bruce and Carol's duplex is pleasantly decorated in a minimalist sort of way, the tour Bruce proudly gives me of the attic, basement, and oversized garage reveals that he by no means shuns material objects. Or at least when it comes to material objects he's found, been given, or scored for next to nothing. "It gives me a sense of security to know that if our toaster breaks, I have a couple of perfectly good ones waiting in reserve, ready to go," he says as he shows me a shelf full of toasters he's found set out in the neighbors' trash on his daily walks or picked up at yard sales or auctions for a dollar or two.

It occurs to me during the tour that Jackson has—through his scavenging and bargain hunting—fully stocked a personal department store as well as a supermarket for himself and Carol. There's the Mormon-worthy food pantry in the basement, the "mattress department" in the garage, and an assortment of furniture, appliances, clothing, and other housewares organized along both sides of a series of passageways, kind of like a topsy-turvy Target store.

"If you have the space—which we do—it's wasteful to throw good things out and costs nothing to hang on to them." And, in fact, sometimes hanging on to things you get for free or very little can pay big dividends: A 1966 Volkswagen Beetle he paid $400 for almost twenty-five years ago—and keeps like a corpse in the morgue under a white sheet in his garage—is now worth upward of $10,000. Not a bad investment of a little money and storage space.

Jackson is clearly what I call a "creative repurposer"—someone who reuses (again and again and again) things that most people would simply throw away. He proudly shows me a massive jar filled with leftover soap slivers (see photo on page 170) that he repurposes in a number of ways, including displaying a collection of some of the more colorful ones—which at first glance I mistook for beautiful seashells—in the base of a lamp in his living room. "I bought it (the jar of soap slivers) at a rummage sale for 25 cents, and I like to keep it mostly for inspiration. I would love to meet the person who saved them all!" he says with genuine enthusiasm.

He instructs me on how you can save broken wooden clothespins (the spring variety) and eventually come up with enough replacement parts to piece them back together. "Two broken ones are all that are needed to make one good one."

Then there are the boxes filled with outdated wall calendars neatly filed in his attic by year. "Collector's items?" I ask.

"No. Don't you know? And you call yourself a cheapskate," he says with another sly smile and a roll of his eyes. Bruce explains that all calendars will *eventually* become current again, if you just hang on to them long enough (see www.whencanireusethiscalendar.com). One of Bruce's holiday traditions following Thanksgiving dinner is to supply everyone in the family with an "old" calendar that will once again be current in the upcoming new year. In a rather melancholy tone, Bruce points out that he will not be saving the calendars from this year, 2012, since it's a leap year and they will not be usable again for another twenty-eight years. "I think it's safe to say that I won't be needing a calendar by then," he says, filing away the last of those he's taken out of the boxes to proudly show me.

Like many "cheapskates" I've met, Jackson is anything *but* cheap when it comes to charity and helping others. In addition to his volunteer work, Bruce Jackson strikes me as the kind of "good neighbor" anyone would be thankful and fortunate to have. And although he doesn't brag about it, I discover that he donates about 20 percent of his modest annual income to a variety of charities, and most of his estate is scheduled to go to charity as well. "I've always tried to follow the words of Gandhi," he says: *"Live simply so others may simply live."*

As I prepare to leave his house the next morning, Bruce has laid out on the sofa a few parting gifts for me as well: an extra-large jacket and shirt that he bought at a yard sale for $1 apiece but that turned out to be a little too roomy for him; two boxes of cereal quite a bit past their expiration dates that he picked up at the local salvage grocery store; and a 2002 "Countdown to Victory!" calendar from the Democratic National Committee.

Yep, your 2002 calendar—if you still have it in your attic—will be current again in 2013. Who knew? Well, Bruce Jackson, for one.

CHAPTER 7

Surviving the Medical Maelstrom

For anyone considering retirement or already retired, health care—including assisted living and long-term care—is likely to be a top-of-mind concern. Particularly if you're planning to retire before age sixty-five, the age at which you probably currently qualify for Medicare, health-care insurance premiums and out-of-pocket expenses may well be your single largest annual expense. And even if you are enrolled in Medicare, supplemental coverage and other costs borne by Medicare recipients are going to be major line items in your retirement budget.

When it comes to the topic of the US health-care system, I've found that there are two types of people: those who believe that America has a true, full-blown, and ever-worsening crisis when it comes to the rising costs of health care, and those who have never had to find and pay for health-care coverage out of their own pockets.

Hopefully you are among the latter group and will always remain so, or otherwise you'll quickly come to appreciate why "crisis" is, if anything, an understatement when describing the status of affordable health care in America. According to data from the Kaiser Family Foundation and the US Bureau of Labor Statistics, between 1999 and 2009, family health-care insurance premiums rose by more than 130 percent, while US worker earnings rose by just 38 percent during the same period.

But there are really two health-care crises going on in America, and I'd like to briefly address both in this chapter, because both deserve serious consideration if you plan to retire better, earlier, and happier.

In addition to the challenge of paying for health-care insurance and other associated medical costs, the second health-care crisis confronting the United States is the fact that we seem hell-bent on doing everything we can to destroy our health by the lifestyle choices so many Americans make. We're not helping matters when it comes to increasing our self-inflicted "health repair" costs. More than one-third of all Americans are now classified as "obese," and another third are officially "overweight," according the Centers for Disease Control and Prevention (CDC), representing roughly a 50 percent increase in comparable rates since 1980.

It's sort of like a race: which will be supersized faster, our health-care costs or our waistlines? To retire the cheapskate way, you need to plan for and address both of these health-care crises in your own life. The good news is, it is indeed possible to survive the medical maelstrom, although it is a serious cheapskate challenge.

"Too Young for Medicare, and Too Old for Women to Care"

– – – – – – – –

That's one of my favorite quotes from one of my favorite living philosophers, Kinky Friedman, Texas's own comedian-musician-author-politician laureate. He's describing what he calls "the worst of all possible ages." And, at least in my case, it's proven true.

I admit that for many years I didn't understand or appreciate why some people seemed so concerned about the cost of health care. Ever since graduating from college, I'd been covered under the health plans provided by my employers, which they paid for in full. I had no idea how much my employer paid for that coverage, nor did I really care. If I sometimes needed to shell out a $10 co-payment when I saw the doctor or filled a prescription, it was no big deal, even for a cheapskate like me.

It wasn't until I left my last "real job" at the age of forty-seven in order to pursue my selfish employment as a writer that I came to appreciate why so many people are in a state of panic over the cost of health care in the United States. And I'm not talking just about people with limited incomes, or the chronically ill, or those who are unemployed. Much to our horror, Denise and I discovered that the health-care crisis stands to financially ruin even middle-class people like us, folks who have benefited from being born into economically sound families and have worked hard their whole adult lives (and much of our childhoods!) to earn a good living, people who are educated, financially responsible, and who have built a not-insignificant financial safety net.

Yet what we found when I prepared to leave my last regular job was that our health care, at best, would cost us each month as much as or more than we used to pay for our home mortgage. And—if we were unlucky—our health-care costs could potentially bankrupt us. This, even though we owned a home free and clear, had considerable savings and other investments, and didn't owe a dime in debt. Here we'd always thought that health care was just something poor people struggled to afford.

Since my wife's employer offers no health-care plan whatsoever for employees working in her capacity (she's an adjunct instructor at a community college), following my resignation, we continued our health insurance through the Consolidated Omnibus Budget Reconciliation Act of 1985, commonly referred to as COBRA. Under that law, most employers with group health plans must offer employees the option of temporarily continuing (for up to eighteen months) their group health-care coverage under their employer's plan if coverage would otherwise end. However, if you elect to continue coverage under COBRA, the ex-employee—and not the employer—is now responsible for paying the entire monthly premium, plus an administrative surcharge for good measure.

At almost $1,000 per month in premiums (all of which we needed to pay for ourselves), plus various deductibles, co-pays, and the like, I began to realize what a valuable employer-provided benefit I'd been taking for granted all these years. Of course, employers haven't always paid such astronomical amounts for their employee health plans. The skyrocketing cost of health care in the United States is the reason why many employers are now dropping their plans for employees altogether or are now requiring employees to bear a larger and larger burden of the costs themselves. And employers who continue to provide gratis (or even subsidized) health-care coverage to employees after they retire—a practice that in generations past was very common—are now about as rare as a proctologist who also practices dentistry.

So, for the first eighteen months after leaving my former position (i.e., the period when we were entitled to continue coverage under COBRA, at our own expense), we were spending about $16,000 per year in premiums, deductibles, co-pays, and medical costs not covered by insurance, and that was just for the two of us.

But when our COBRA coverage finally ran out, that's when things got really bad. Because my wife has had some fairly serious medical problems in the past—some of which are ongoing—the Yeagers were declared, in essence, "uninsurable at any price," at least in terms of being able to buy a policy on the open market that would cover "preexisting conditions," of which Denise had several.

I remember the day that news finally sank in: I felt like I'd just undergone groin surgery without anesthesia. I simply couldn't believe that two hardworking, tax-paying, financially responsible, patriotic Americans—with an ability to pay at least a reasonable sum for coverage—were being denied coverage *specifically because* of the fact that, with Denise's medical background, it was likely that she would actually need some medical assistance in the future! It's like the old line about being able to qualify for a bank loan only if you really don't need one.

Fortunately, the state of Maryland, where we live, has a state-mandated "risk pool"—an "insurer of last resort," if you will—which is required under law to accept anyone (regardless of preexisting conditions), provided that you are able to pay whatever premiums they mandate and that you never allow coverage to lapse. We opted for a policy with the highest possible annual deductible (paying the first $5,000 or so of claims ourselves), with coverage then kicking in to varying degrees after that.

The advantage of these high-deductible health plans (HDHPs) is that they traditionally come with the lowest monthly premiums. Nonetheless, in the five years we've been enrolled under the plan, the premiums have more than doubled, the deductible amounts have steadily increased, and the amounts and items covered under the plan continue to decline.

Every July, when the policy comes up for renewal and they announce the new terms and cost of the plan, I feel like a little helpless kid at Christmastime. You know, like before you really understood money and the price of things. When you simply stood in front of a store cashier with your homemade Tandy Leather wallet held wide open, trusting that the cashier would take the right amount out of your billfold for the gifts you were buying for Mom and Dad. But there is no other option available to us, other than going uninsured or reentering the traditional workforce with the hopes of finding an employer who provides coverage.

Last year, nearly half of our total net household spending was for health care. And God forbid if we exhaust the lifetime cap on the plan we're currently covered under before we qualify for Medicare. Then it's conceivable that continued medical problems could rip through our assets and even force us into bankruptcy, just as health problems are the primary contributors to more than 60 percent of all US personal bankruptcies, according to a 2007 study by Harvard researchers. Yep, the Yeagers are now convinced that the health-care crisis in America is for real.

All that said, what I've just described—as costly as it might be—is still the most common cheapskate prescription for handling health care if you decide to retire before qualifying for Medicare, and if you don't have the luxury of an employer who will continue to provide you with coverage after you've retired. Nearly all the early-retired cheapskates I've spoken with have opted for the most affordable HDHP they can find, and then plan in advance to cover the annual deductible amounts out of their savings.

To take at least a little bit of a bite out of the cost of being insured under an HDHP, it usually makes sense to also set up a health savings account (HSA), a special tax-advantaged medical savings account available specifically for people enrolled in an HDHP. Funds deposited into an HSA are not subject to federal income tax at the time of deposit and can be used to pay qualified medical expenses at any time without federal tax liability or penalty. See IRS Publication 969, *Health Savings Accounts and Other Tax-Favored Health Plans*, for more information.

"We don't like it [having such high health-care costs and an HDHP], but at least we can live with it . . . no pun intended. Since we don't have any debt hanging over our heads and we know we have enough in savings to cover the maximum amounts we could be forced to pay out of our own pocket every year, a high-deductible plan is the best of all the bad choices for us," says Miser Adviser Adam Bing. "Because of the way we live, we can afford to take on more of the risk ourselves. I can't imagine what we'd do if it wasn't for that fact . . . if we just couldn't afford it, period. It's really just like having an ultimate safety net, so that if we have some catastrophic medical expenses, there'll at least be some coverage to hopefully stave off bankruptcy. It's a real pisser, though."

I thought Adam's last comment nicely summarized the available health-care options for early retirees and self-employed Americans, even for those of us nonurologists.

There's a very useful calculator tool on the AARP website that helps you figure out whether a high-deductible health plan and a health savings account are better options for you than other more traditional health plans. You can find it here at www.aarp.org/health/medicare-insurance /hsa_calculator.

Cheapskate Retirement Principle #12

If you retire before you're eligible for Medicare (typically age sixty-five), a high-deductible health plan (HDHP) and a health savings account (HSA) may very well be your best option for health-care coverage, particularly if you're a true cheapskate and have no debt and a sufficient financial safety net to pay deductible amounts and other out-of-pocket expenses. But even then, it ain't cheap.

Medicare Basics: Do You Want the Soup or an Eggroll?

Will you still need me, will you still feed me, when I'm sixty-four? Well, we'll see about that. But when you turn sixty-five (under current law), most Americans are entitled to receive some significant assistance when it comes to caring for their health and covering at least some of their medical expenses.

That's the age at which most Americans qualify to begin receiving Medicare, the health insurance program run by the federal government for older people, as well as some younger people with disabilities and other conditions. In 2011, one baby boomer became eligible for Medicare every eight seconds!

☞ *You might need a Cheapskate Intervention if you've ever tried ordering a Medicare donut hole at Dunkin' Donuts, thinking it's some sort of healthier high-fiber snack.*

The good news is that the benefits under Medicare can be significant, and the costs relatively inexpensive, at least when compared to buying comparable health insurance coverage on the open market, as discussed above. The bad news is that the Medicare system is complicated, so you need to take the time to research it carefully and understand how it applies to you and your individual situation. Here are some resources to use in your research:

- The official **US government website for Medicare** (www.Medicare.gov) does a good job of explaining what is by every measure a complicated program and allows you to compare and enroll for some coverages online (including Medicare Part A, via a link to the Social Security Administration website). You can also download a free copy of the official US government handbook (updated annually) entitled *Medicare & You.*
- The free AARP booklet entitled **Understanding Medicare: What You Need to Know** (available on the AARP website, www.AARP.org, or by requesting a copy by mail) is a very helpful primer on the topic.
- Assuming that you're employed and have had health-care coverage prior to age sixty-five, be sure to talk with

your employer's benefits administrator in advance of your sixty-fifth birthday to determine how any employer-provided health-care plans may impact your decisions and options regarding participation in Medicare.

• And finally, talk with a counselor through the **State Health Insurance Assistance Program** (www.ship talk.org); this a free, nonprofit, nationwide network of health insurance counselors who can advise you on how Medicare and other insurance options may apply to your particular situation, and they do so without trying to sell you anything!

Without attempting even a rudimentary explanation of the *entire* Medicare system, here are a few important takeaway points from the cheapskate's perspective:

1. Medicare has four "parts" or "plans," cleverly titled **Parts A, B, C, and D**. I find it helpful to think of Medicare as a Chinese menu, only more confusing, with very few prices listed, and no mu shu pork as an option.

2. **Medicare Part A** is often referred to as "hospital coverage," as it primarily covers nursing care and hospital stays, but not doctors' fees. Most Americans are entitled to receive Part A coverage for free when they turn sixty-five, having paid for it out of payroll taxes during their (or their spouse's) working years. It's like the Chinese tea they automatically serve you without charge as soon

as you sit down at the table. But remember that Part A coverage is limited: there is a yearly deductible you must meet for hospitalization costs ($1,156 in 2012) if you use it, and even then it pays only a portion of your Medicare-approved inpatient costs and only for limited periods of time.

3. **Medicare Part B** is optional, like an eggroll, and covers some of the costs not covered by Part A, including a portion of some doctors' visits, some medical equipment, some lab tests, some home health care . . . in other words, some of this and some of that, but not everything. You may want to opt out of Part B if you still have health insurance through an employer, union, spouse, or the like, although if you do opt out and then want to enroll later, you may have to pay a higher premium. Part B premiums, which are often deducted directly from recipients' Social Security checks (with their approval, of course), are currently quite reasonable (a standard rate of $99.90 per month in 2012). So from a cheapskate's perspective, Part B coverage is a pretty good value—again, like an eggroll—unless you already have comparable coverage. But even then, there is an annual deductible you must pay (currently $140) and other limitations.

4. If you're already confused, hang on to your chopsticks, 'cause you ain't seen nothin' yet. **Medicare Part C** is a slate of optional plans—sometimes known as "Medi-

care Advantage" or "Medicare Health" plans—offered through private insurance companies that are approved by Medicare. If you want to enroll in a Part C plan, you must first be enrolled in both Part A and Part B. The cost of Part C coverage varies based on all types of things but generally gives you some additional coverages (sometimes including vision and dental, and often at least some prescription drug coverage—but check the terms of the policy carefully) and smaller co-pay amounts than traditional Medicare. Some Part C plans work like an HMO (health maintenance organization), which can lock you into using just certain doctors and facilities, so that can be a potential drawback for some patients.

5. And that brings us to **Medicare Part D**, which at least makes sense in that Part "D" is all about "drugs" (which you probably need to go along with your sake by this point). So-called Medicare Part D prescription drug plans are actually many different plans provided through insurers and other companies working with Medicare to provide some insurance coverage for brand-name and generic prescription drugs. To enroll in a Part D plan, you must already be enrolled in Part A and Part B (and, no, you cannot order the wonton soup with that). At the same time, keep in mind that if you are covered under a Part C plan, you may already have some prescription drug benefits and may not need a Part D plan. While plans vary, with Part D, each month you pay a premium

(estimated by the federal government to average about $38 per month in 2012, more for wealthier households). You may also have to pay a yearly deductible (averaging $320 in 2012), before coverage kicks in. And, even once coverage starts, under most plans the insurance company picks up only part of the tab, requiring some type of co-pay from the patient.

Confused? Well, sit back and have another potsticker, because now comes the infamous "donut hole." In most Part D plans, there is a coverage gap—aka the "donut hole"—after you reach a certain spending limit (i.e., what you and your insurer combined have paid). In 2012, that limit is $2,930, after which Medicare Part D stops paying. From that point until you've spent $4,550 on prescription drugs for the year, the burden is on you to pay for your own meds. However, at least for 2012, there is a special 50 percent discount for covered brand-name drugs, and plans will pay 14 percent of the cost of covered generic drugs as a way of helping you swallow the donut hole without choking on it. Once you've exceed the $4,550 amount, then, thankfully, "catastrophic coverage" kicks in, and Medicare pays about 95 percent of all your prescription drug costs for the rest of the year . . . after which the whole cycle begins again.

6. And now a word about **Medigap** coverage, or so called "Medicare Supplement Insurance." This is insurance sold by private companies that helps to pay for certain

costs not covered by Medicare (hence "gaps"), like co-payments, deductibles, and hospice care coinsurance. It's available only to people who are covered by Part A and Part B; if you're covered by Part C, you are ineligible to purchase Medigap coverage (and no fortune cookie for you!). As you'll no doubt guess by now, there are many different types of Medigap policies (eleven, to be exact, each designed like a mini–Chinese menu all its own) covering specific types and groups of gaps, and by law you can buy only one of these plans.

So, there you have it: Medicare in a lychee nutshell. I don't blame you if you feel like a Peking duck who's just been decapitated.

Two final topics deserve at least a brief mention here: Medicaid coverage and long-term care insurance, unrelated but both important.

Medicaid—unlike Medicare, which is available to every US citizen sixty-five years or older, regardless of income or assets—is available only to people with low incomes, limited resources, or certain disabilities or diseases. Although Medicaid is a federal program, it is administered through each state individually, and Medicaid programs (including which health-care services are covered) vary greatly from state to state. To see if you qualify for Medicaid and what assistance might be available to you, you need to contact your state's Medicaid program. The federal government website www.Benefits.gov can direct you to your state's program and provide more general information.

And as for the advisability of securing **long-term care insurance**—sometimes called "nursing home insurance"—again, there's not a single "right answer" for everyone, although generally prevailing opinions among financial experts and cheapskates alike is that it's probably a wise expenditure of funds for only a limited range of people. Statistically, the odds are not great that most people will spend a protracted period of time in a nursing facility. In fact, two-thirds of men and one-third of women age sixty-five and older will never spend a single day in a nursing facility, and even then, most stays are relatively brief.

☞ *You might need a Cheapskate Intervention if, instead of buying long-term care insurance, you send away for a do-it-yourself cryonics kit you saw advertised on late-night TV.*

Couple this with the high premiums paid for long-term care policies (particularly for individuals at an age when coverage is more desirable) and the notorious number of limitations and loopholes in many policies, and, at a minimum, let the buyer beware. In short, if you're very wealthy, you can probably afford the price of nursing care should you need it, and if you're of limited financial means, you probably cannot afford the cost of the long-term care premiums. You should also know that under Medicaid laws, there is virtually no chance of you being denied access to nursing facilities and thrown out onto the street because of an inability to pay. Obviously, things like your family situation, housing arrangements, estate/legacy plans, and even the terms of your living will can have an impact on your decision regarding long-term care insurance.

That said, some financial advisers do suggest that if you have net assets worth between $300,000 and $500,000 (not including the equity in your home), you *might* consider purchasing long-term care insurance as a prudent investment, provided that you read all of the fine print in the policy first.

Cheapskate Retirement Principle #13

When it comes to Medicare and health-care options for those sixty-five years and older, there are far too many variables to prescribe a one-size-fits-all plan, a strategy that is right for everyone. For many, enrolling in Medicare Parts A, B, and D can be a good value, even for a cheapskate. And depending on your medical and financial situation, some supplemental or Medigap insurance may be a sound investment as well. The best advice is to become knowledgeable about the myriad options available and understand how they relate to your particular financial and health-care needs.

Get Frugally Fit and Stay That Way

I speak to a lot of groups of young people, many of them still in high school or junior high, about money and how to spend and manage it wisely. A centerpiece of that particular stump speech is what I bill as "the single, most important piece of financial advice you'll ever hear." I can always see some kids perking up at that point in my presentation, thinking, perhaps, that I'm about to reveal a secret promotional code that will get them a free Xbox or iPad or SketRobo.

No—sorry to disappoint, kids—but the words of cheapskate wisdom I have to impart are exactly those spoken by Miser Adviser Wanda Adams (see pages 213–219): *"If you aren't healthy, work to get healthier. And if you are healthy, work to stay that way."* I then go on to explain why that health advice is such important financial advice, not only when it comes to helping to avoid expensive health-care and health-repair costs during your lifetime, but also when it comes to understanding that you need to maintain your health so that you can work and generate income as needed.

But whether you're eighteen or eighty, I'd still offer the exact same advice, and it's an even more critical consideration as you prepare for and live in retirement.

I know, I know, I know. You already have health and medical problems, maybe even some you were born with and others that are also no fault of your own. The fact is, most people do, especially those of us who are baby boomers or older. However, that shouldn't be an excuse to ignore

Wanda's advice and simply abandon any attempt to constantly, throughout your entire life, improve upon and maintain your *optimum* health as much as possible.

Note that I use the word "optimum," and not "perfect" or "good" or even "satisfactory." The idea is that we all have different physical limitations, as well as health problems and potential problems, some of which we can't do anything about. But that doesn't mean we can't work to maintain what is, for each of us, our "optimum health" (i.e., as good as it can be, given the particulars of your situation).

Obviously, there are no guarantees when it comes to the efforts you put into maintaining your optimum health and the actual results. To wit: I go for a bicycle ride almost every day, which I know for certain saves me some gas money since I run fewer errands by car, and which is apparently one of the reasons why my cardiovascular and general level of fitness is considered quite strong for a man of my age. That said, if one day I'm struck and killed or injured by a car while riding my bike, you could argue that my effort to maintain "optimum health" actually ended up harming my health. Clearly, though, arguments like that are a fool's errand, since life is filled with risks and uncertain outcomes (e.g., I could just as well be injured in an auto accident while driving a car, which provides virtually no fitness benefits), and the best you can ever do is simply play the odds.

But speaking of playing the odds, so many of the medical maladies currently plaguing Americans *are* in fact things that we can, in our own lives, mitigate through our lifestyle choices and personal behavior. The odds are heavily in your favor when it comes to being able to avoid—or at least reduce the impact/likelihood of—so-called "preventable health threats" simply by altering the way you live . . . that's why they're considered "preventable"! According to the Centers for Disease Control and Prevention (CDC), the following top-six health threats are all ones for which an ounce of prevention is worth many pounds of cure:

Threat	Preventative Measures
#1—HEART DISEASE The leading cause of death among Americans, both men and women.	• Don't smoke • Eat a healthy diet • Exercise regularly • Limit alcohol • Maintain a healthy weight • Manage stress • **Manage chronic conditions like high cholesterol, high blood pressure, and diabetes**
#2—CANCER Various types are considered preventable, including lung cancer, skin cancer, prostate cancer, and colorectal cancer.	• Don't smoke • Maintain a healthy weight • Exercise regularly • Eat a healthy diet • Use sun protection/avoid sun • Limit alcohol • **Early detection/screening**

Threat	Preventative Measures
#3—MOTOR VEHICLE ACCIDENTS	• Use common sense • Obey all traffic laws • Wear your seat belt • No texting or cell phone use while driving • Don't drive while intoxicated or sleepy
#4—CHRONIC LOWER RESPIRATORY DISEASE Chronic lung conditions, including bronchitis and emphysema.	• Don't smoke • Avoid environmental pollutants • Prevent respiratory infections by washing your hands often and getting a **yearly flu vaccination**
#5—STROKE Some factors can't be controlled—like family history, age, and race—but some can.	• Don't smoke • Eat a healthy diet • Exercise regularly • Maintain a healthy weight • Limit alcohol • **Manage chronic conditions like high cholesterol, high blood pressure, and diabetes**
#6—TYPE 2 DIABETES Poorly controlled diabetes can lead to heart disease, eye problems, nerve damage, and other complications.	• Eat a healthy diet • Exercise regularly • Maintain a healthy weight

Based on data from the Centers for Disease Control and Prevention at www.CDC.gov

Gee, what do you notice about that list? Do you see any trends? Not smoking, limiting alcohol consumption, and maintaining a healthy weight through diet and exercise seem to pop up over and over again, don't they? And, of course, doing any of those things is not costly, at least if you do them the cheapskate way. In fact, two items on the list—not smoking and not drinking alcohol (or drinking less of it)—will actually *save* you money.

Of all the preventative measures listed by the CDC, only those few items listed in **bold** require the possible expenditure of money on health-care providers or medications. Everything else on the list is something that you can do yourself for little or no additional expense, just by how you behave and the choices you make. But that's the thing, only *you* can do it; nobody else can do it for you.

When it comes to eating healthy, cheapskates generally agree that the healthiest diet you can eat just happens to be one that costs the least, particularly if you're a smart shopper and plan your menus around the healthiest food choices that are on sale at the grocery store each week (aka "the loss leaders"). When you think about it, many of the healthiest foods you can eat—those things we should be eating the most of, according to the good old USDA "food pyramid" (www.mypyramid.gov)—cost the least. I'm talking about things like whole grains, legumes, and fresh fruits and vegetables, particularly when you buy them in season. Conversely, many of the least healthy foods (at least if eaten in large quantities), such as red meat, fatty dairy products, and many processed foods that are high in saturated and trans fats, typically cost the most.

No, I'm not suggesting that everyone should become a vegetarian, nor am I a vegetarian myself. But eating lower on the food chain—even when it comes to things like choosing relatively inexpensive poultry over costlier red meat—and eating less meat in general, is going to result in both a better diet and a bigger bank account. The same is true if you take the time to prepare more foods for yourself rather than relying on restaurants or fast food, or on many notoriously costly and unhealthy processed or prepared foods.

I still stand by my claim as I described it in my first book, *The Ultimate Cheapskate's Road Map to True Riches*, that I can walk into almost any supermarket in America and put together a delicious, nutritious dinner consisting entirely of ingredients costing under $1 per pound, including on-sale items, but without using coupons. And that book was published in 2007, when grocery prices were about 12 percent lower than today.

If you don't believe me, here's a list of fifty healthy foods I've purchased in the past year (yes, a number of them were super store specials, but I didn't use any coupons) for $1 a pound or less. And remember, I live in the Washington, DC, metropolitan area, with one of the highest costs of living—and of groceries!—in the country:

- *Apples*—One a day keeps the cheapskate away.
- *Asparagus*—HUGE store special at 99 cents a pound

during Easter week. I bought ten pounds, blanched it, and then froze it.

- *Bananas*—Potassium for pennies.
- *Barley*—A tasty alternative to rice and potatoes.
- *Beans*—Canned or dried—kidney, pinto, navy, black, red, and many more.
- *Bok choy*—Steam and serve with a little soy sauce.
- *Broccoli*—Yes, a store special. Usually closer to $2 a pound.
- *Bulgar wheat*—Try it in pilaf or a tabbouleh salad.
- *Cabbage*—Green and red—I like mine fried.
- *Cantaloupe?*—No, sorry, I can't; I'm already married.
- *Carrots*—Raw or steamed; rich in carotenes, a healthy antioxidant.
- *Celery*—Stir-fry it for a change.
- *Chicken*—Whole or various parts, on sale.
- *Chickpeas*—AKA garbanzo beans—mash 'em up as a healthy sandwich spread.
- *Cornmeal*—"Polenta" is all the rage these days, but I loved it forty years ago when Mom called it "cornmeal mush."
- *Cucumbers*—Try peeling, seeding, and steaming with a little butter and salt.
- *Daikon radish*—My new favorite raw veggie.
- *Eggs*—Don't overdo them, but eggs provide high-quality protein and still cost about $1 a pound.
- *Grapefruit*—Bake with a little brown sugar on top for a healthy dessert.

- *Grapes*—Store special at 99 cents a pound.
- *Green beans*—Frozen—but fresh are sometimes on sale for under $1 a pound in season.
- *Greens*—Kale, mustard, turnip, and collard greens are rich in vitamins and a good source of fiber.
- *Lentils*—Perhaps the perfect food—healthy, cheap, and versatile (think soups, salads, sandwich spreads—and those are only some of the "s" possibilities).
- *Liver*—Chicken livers usually cost under $1 a pound, and sometimes beef and pork liver can be found in the DMZ ("dollar maximum zone").
- *Mangoes*—High in fiber and vitamins A, B_6, and C.
- *Milk*—Yep, on a per-pound basis, milk still costs well under $1 a pound.
- *Napa cabbage*—Delicious steamed or raw in a salad.
- *Oatmeal*—The good old-fashioned "slow cooking" kind . . . that takes all of five minutes.
- *Onions*—Try baking them whole in a cream sauce.
- *Oranges*—Frequent sale price when in season.
- *Pasta*—Store special at 89 cents a pound—I nearly bought them out!
- *Peanut butter*—Special sale price, but stock up because it usually has a long shelf life.
- *Pork*—Inexpensive cuts of pork frequently go on sale for 99 cents a pound or less; sometime even ham during the holidays.
- *Potatoes*—White and red—baked, mashed, boiled, broiled, steamed.

- *Pumpkin*—Yes, you can eat the same ones you buy as holiday decorations, and they usually cost under 50 cents a pound.
- *Rice*—White for under $1 a pound; brown, a little more expensive but better for you.
- *Rutabagas*—Hated them as a kid; can't get enough of them now.
- *Sour cream*—16-ounce container for 99 cents on sale, but long shelf life, so stock up. My cucumber awaits.
- *Spinach*—Frozen (but Popeye doesn't care).
- *Split peas*—Add a ham bone and make the ultimate comfort soup.
- *Squash*—Try baking acorn squash with a little brown sugar.
- *Sweet corn*—Canned—or fresh on the cob in season.
- *Tomatoes*—Canned—canned are often better than fresh to use in cooking, but occasionally you can find fresh on sale for under a buck in season, too.
- *Turkey*—A popular bargain-priced loss leader around the holidays—buy an extra bird and freeze it for later.
- *Turnips*—Make me think of my grandparents, who always grew them.
- *Watermelon*—Whole, in-season melons can sometimes cost less than 20 cents a pound if they're on sale and you find a big one.
- *Wine*—Well, at least the stuff I drink—5-liter box

(approximately eleven pounds) for about ten bucks,
on sale. (By the way, the beer I drink is even less
expensive per pound.)
- *Yams/sweet potatoes*—One of the healthiest foods
you can eat, and usually available year-round for
under $1 a pound.
- *Yogurt*—8-ounce containers on sale two for $1.
- *Zucchini*—Okay, they're a type of squash (above).
But I love them so much they deserve their own
place on the list.

As for staying in shape by getting regular exercise, no
need to spend money on expensive health club memberships
or personal trainers. In fact, my advice to most people who
belong to a gym is to go to their local thrift store and buy a
used bicycle, then pedal it on over to the gym and cancel
their membership; use the bike—or walk—for close-by errands (like Bruce Jackson's one-mile challenge), and you'll
get plenty of exercise while saving on both gas and gym
membership dues.

"The first time I did it, I thought I was going to die,"
sixty-seven-year-old Pam Martyr told me about her initial
sojourn to the corner grocery store by foot instead of by car,
a journey of not quite a mile and a quarter round-trip. "And
the second time I did it two days later, I wished I would die!
My feet and legs were still sore from the first trip. But, you
know, after that it got easier every time, and now I don't

even think about it." Pam, who is overweight and diabetic, bought a lightweight two-wheeled cart ("at a yard sale!") to haul her groceries home with her, and has lost "ten pounds without even trying" since she started her walks to the grocery store just three short months ago.

☞ *You might need a Cheapskate Intervention if your idea of an aerobic workout is getting up for yet another plateful at Golden Corral.*

Simply by taking the time to do more things for yourself (see Chapter 8), you'll save money and in many instances get the physical workout you need. Here's a table (compliments of my first book) that shows the calories burned, muscle groups used, and estimated dollars saved by performing simple everyday chores yourself:

Activity	Savings[1]	Calories[2]	Muscles Used[3]
Wash your own car	$15	610	B, UA, LL, A
Cut your own grass	$40	490	T, B, LL, UA, LA
Walk instead of taxi (4 miles)	$8	245	T, B, LL
Run instead of taxi (6 miles)	$12	1,080	T, B, LL
Bicycle instead of taxi (14 miles)	$28	980	T, B, LL, LA
Paint your own house	$25	410	B, UA, LA, A
Shovel your own snow	$25	490	T, B, LL, UA, LA
Rake your own leaves	$15	350	T, B, LL, UA, LA, A

Activity	Savings[1]	Calories[2]	Muscles Used[3]
Clean your own house	$20	245	T, B, LL, UA, LA
Do your own gardening	$20	330	B, UA, LA
Clean your own gutters	$20	410	B, UA, LA
Cut your own firewood	$25	490	B, UA, LA

[1] Estimated savings are for one hour of labor costs.
[2] Calories burned are based on a 180-pound person performing the activity for one hour. Based on the *Compendium of Physical Activities: An Update of Activity Codes and MET Intensities.* From the official journal of the American College of Sports Medicine: *Medicine & Science in Sports & Exercise,* September 2000.
[3] Muscle group abbreviations: B, back; T, thighs; LL, lower legs; UA, upper arms/shoulders; LA, lower arms; A, abdominals.

But even if you do spring for a health club membership or need the motivation provided by a personal trainer, it's money well spent when it comes to saving on health care and health repair further down the road. Many commercial health clubs provide discounts for seniors (including Gold's Gym with an AARP membership card), as do YMCAs. Community colleges and senior citizen centers, as well as parks and recreation departments, often offer health and fitness programs and facilities for little or no charge.

Of course, before undertaking any diet or exercise program, always consult your doctor first. Be sure to mention that you've been diagnosed as a Chronic Cheapskate, so that he or she knows the price range of the treatment options you're looking for.

Cheapskate Retirement Principle #14

The time you invest in maintaining your health will likely yield a greater financial return in the form of future savings than spending the same number of hours working to pay for health-care insurance and health-repair costs further down the road. In other words, spend at least as much time taking care of your health as you spend time earning money to pay for health care.

SOME CHEAPSKATE ALTERNATIVES TO TRADITIONAL HEALTH AND LONG-TERM CARE

- **Medical Vacations:** With baby boomers not getting any younger and medical care not getting any cheaper, "medical vacations" are becoming one of the fastest-growing segments of the travel industry. Each year an estimated half a million Americans travel outside the United States to have medical procedures—everything from liver transplants and heart surgery to plastic surgery and dental work—performed in other countries, where they often cost considerably less and where the quality of care is at least on a par with that in the States.

In many cases, the savings can be significant, perhaps only a third of the cost of the same procedure in the United States, and that's after factoring in airfare/travel and lodging expenses during any recovery time.

Countries catering to medical tourists include India, the Philippines, Costa Rica, Malaysia, Singapore, Brazil, Argentina, Mexico, and Thailand. Some US travel agencies even specialize in arranging medical vacations, including PlanetHospital (www.Planet Hospital.com), which offers the option of having a US doctor travel overseas with you to perform the procedure in a country where hospital and other costs are significantly lower.

You can check the website of the Joint Commission of Accreditation of Healthcare Organizations for a list of accredited health-care facilities in different countries (www.jointcommissioninternationaljournal .org). Also, check out the book *Patients Beyond Borders: Everybody's Guide to Affordable, World-Class Medical Tourism*, by Josef Woodman.

Of course, moving permanently or semipermanently to another country (see Chapter 6) may, in many cases, allow you to participate in that country's health-care system, which in nearly every instance is likely to cost considerably less than health care here in the United States, since per capita health-care spending in America is nearly double that of any other developed country . . . yet our life expectancy in the United States is among the lowest of any developed country (per World Health Organization data). Go figure.

- **Planning Ahead to Stay in Your Own Home as Long (and as Inexpensively) as Possible:** Do you remember the old TV show *Frasier,* starring Kelsey Grammer, the show with the live-in health-care provider named Daphne Moon? Well, as part of their possible longer-term care strategies, many cheapskates we've met in this book—for example, the Burdens, the Allens (profiled on pages 251–260), and even the Yeagers—have created small apartment units within their homes that may help to reduce in-home assisted-living expenses by providing caregivers with a free place to live, as part of a compensation package. Obviously, local zoning laws and other regulations may apply, but it's something to consider when shopping for a home. Of course, if that time ever comes for me, I'll be looking to recruit a comely young caregiver like Daphne Moon, although I somehow think I'll deservedly end up with a live-in Nurse Ratched like in *One Flew over the Cuckoo's Nest.*

- **Joining an Old-Hippie Retirement Commune:** If your home doesn't lend itself to creating a space where a caregiver can live if that time comes, check into the growing network of what some call "retirement communes." These are a wide range of shared-housing arrangements, everything from informal house sharing (think *The Golden Girls*) to more structured group facilities, some of which offer nursing and assisted-care services. But the focus is more on community and collective living—with everyone sharing not just in the costs, but in taking care of one another and jointly operating the "commune" as much as possible.

This isn't your grandma's nursing home, I quickly discovered when I visited a facility falling within this category near Morgantown, West Virginia. It was clean, homey, and everyone I met seemed genuinely into the community aspect of their shared living arrangement. It was also relatively inexpensive, with many residents paying about $2,000 per month for a private room with bath and three meals per day, plus access to the home's free around-town shuttle service.

The book *Old Age in a New Age: The Promise of Trans-formative Nursing Homes,* by Beth Baker, is highly recommended, as is the website of the nonprofit National Shared Housing Resource Center (www.nationalshared housing.org). To locate more traditional nursing homes, facilities operated by faith-based and other nonprofit groups, and information on senior housing vouchers and low-income nursing homes subsidized by the US Department of Housing and Urban Development, the following website is helpful:

www.guidetonursinghomes.com/family-resources
/affordable-nursing-homes.html.

- **Physician Aid in Dying:** For more and more people, the final act of health care is deciding—rightfully and legally—the proper ending of their own lives. "Physician aid in dying" (PAD), also called "physician-assisted suicide," is now legal in Oregon, Washington, and Montana, as well as in a number of foreign countries, including Belgium, Germany, Luxembourg, Switzerland, and the Netherlands. Laws vary, but in general the patient must be determined by a doctor(s) and other witnesses to be of sound mind when requesting assisted suicide, and the patient must be diagnosed with a terminal illness. The main difference between PAD and "euthanasia" is who administers the lethal dose of medication; with "euthanasia" (which is illegal in all fifty states and most other countries), a doctor or other third party administers the medication, whereas with PAD, the patient must self-administer the lethal dose.

Some useful nonprofit websites related to the growing "death with dignity" movement include:

www.finalexit.org
www.assistedsuicide.org
www.endoflifechoices.org
and
www.worldrtd.net (the World Federation of
    Right to Die Societies).

The book *Final Exit,* by Derek Humphry, founder of the former Hemlock Society USA, is also an excellent and thought-provoking resource. And for complete information on hospice care (including how to pay for it) and a nationwide directory of hospices, see www.hospice directory.org, a service of the nonprofit Hospice Foundation of America.

WANDA ADAMS

Laughter Is the Best Medicine
(but Long-Term Care Insurance
Might Be a Good Idea, Too)

When you write for a living and the reason why people will, hopefully, buy what you write is because an editor somewhere thinks you're at least somewhat amusing, it's always intimidating—not to mention demoralizing—whenever you meet somebody who's infinitely funnier than you can ever hope to be. For the past thirty years or so, my arch comic nemesis has been Wanda Adams, now a Miser Adviser Emerita, from the Dayton suburb of Trotwood, Ohio.

Many years ago, I learned to leave what little wit I have

checked at the door when Denise and I get together with our longtime friend Wanda. Whether it's Wanda and Denise wildly playing a "dashboard duet" to accompany Billy Joel's "My Life" on the radio while I struggle to keep the car on the road because I'm laughing so hard, or her priceless nonstop stories about the classroom shenanigans she encountered during thirty years of teaching, or the much anticipated "mohel monologue" Wanda delivers at her annual New Year's Eve party as she carefully removes the skin and slices up the gigantic beef stick she serves every year, suffice it to say that Wanda Adams is *stand-up comedian* funny.

And up until she retired from Northmont High School in 2007 at the age of fifty-two, Wanda Adams was also one of the best, most beloved, and most respected teachers at that school. Perhaps ever: in the thirty-year history of Northmont's Teacher of the Year Award, Wanda is the only teacher to ever receive the honor twice, an achievement of which she is understandably proud. "Yep, you could say I broke the mold on that one. Just call me a 'moldbuster,' like a 'dustbuster,' only moldier!" she says with the kind of laugh that instantly makes everyone else in the room crack up along with her.

But the reasons behind Wanda's decision to opt for retiring relatively young—a choice that cost her pretty significantly in reduced pension benefits—are not at all funny. One of Wanda's brothers died suddenly of a heart attack at the age of thirty-six, and another passed away at age fifty-nine after spending four and half years in a vegetative state following a massive heart attack.

"I loved teaching, just loved it," she says. "But I realized that you never know how long you're going to be around, and there were still a lot of things I wanted to do and see outside the classroom. I also wanted to be like one of those really popular TV shows that goes off the air when it's at its peak, before it's lost its edge." I have no doubt that Wanda's premature departure from Northmont was the equivalent of *Seinfeld*'s well-timed exodus from NBC, in more ways than one.

So after three decades of teaching social studies and doing peer counseling at Northmont, Wanda retired earlier than most of her colleagues. That decision resulted in her receiving a pension essentially equivalent to 66 percent of her preretirement salary, as opposed to the 88 percent she would have received if she'd decided to teach five additional years. As a state employee, Wanda is not entitled to receive Social Security, having paid into her teacher's pension plan rather than Social Security during her working years.

"It really wasn't that noticeable," Wanda says about her overnight one-third drop in salary, despite the fact that she now also needs to shoulder much of her own health-care costs. "I'd planned for it, and I've always been frugal. Okay, okay, Jeff, *you* can call me 'cheap' . . . I kind of like the way it sounds when you say it; sort of makes me feel sexy all over. I was raised that way—frugal, I mean, not feeling sexy all over—and I learned from my parents' example. In fact, when it comes to money advice, I always tell people, 'Whatever you do, don't surround yourself with financial idiots . . . it's contagious!'"

Key to Wanda's planning for early retirement was—you guessed it—to retire debt-free. But other than a home mortgage and occasional car loans, Wanda has managed to live most of her life debt-free. The daughter of "Depression baby" parents, she grew up in the Dayton suburbs and attended Wright State University for both her undergraduate and master's degrees. She was a commuter student, continuing to live with her parents while she attended college, an old-school model for getting a college education on-the-cheap, and one that Wanda strongly promoted to her college-bound students when she taught at Northmont. Between part-time jobs, scholarships, grants, and the significant cost savings incurred by living at home, Wanda graduated Summa cum Debt-Free.

"It's pretty hilarious, isn't it, that most students these days can't imagine living at home with their parents when they're in college? So they go away to school, rack up all of these student loans, and after they graduate, they're so broke, *then* they move back home with Mom and Dad! Seems silly to me." Wanda has a good point, since the average four-year college graduate with student loans owes about $27,000 by the time he or she graduates, which, ironically, is almost exactly the cost of four years' worth of room and board at the average public university.

Not being married and living on a public school teacher's salary, Wanda got creative when it came to realizing her long-held dream of homeownership. In the 1980s, she bought a single-level duplex in partnership with another teacher and her husband who also taught at Northmont. Each owner occupied half, and it was a move that allowed Wanda to begin building equity.

Then in 1993, a charming brick Tudor home in Trotwood came on the market, the very same house that Wanda had fantasized about living in ever since she first saw it when she was growing up in the area. It was more than she could afford on her own, but fortunately a fellow Northmont teacher and friend, Dawn Wojcik, was equally as enamored with the lovely home. Wanda sold her half of the duplex to the couple who already owned the other half, and then joined forces with Dawn to buy their dream home together, under a survivorship deed. All expenses for the house are split fifty/fifty, and every year Wanda and Dawn each set aside $2,000 in a special account to make home improvements and other upgrades to the property.

"For us, owning a home together has worked out really well," Wanda says, "particularly since this home allows us each to have our own master-size bedroom and full bath on separate floors, as well as having our separate home offices. The kitchen, dining room, and living room we consider the 'public areas' of our home." Combining their financial efforts has also allowed them to split the cost of property taxes and insurance, as well as other household items, including food, appliances, and shared housewares and furnishings. "There's no way either of us could have afforded this house on our own, let alone have it paid off by the time I retired," Wanda adds.

After she retired, Wanda wanted to try using her ample people skills in some new capacities, and so she launched "Wanda's Waiting" (www.WandasWaiting.com), a classic example of a successful selfish employment venture. A sort of "personal concierge" service, Wanda does everything from waiting in a client's home while they're at work in order to let repairmen in and out, to doing people's shopping and other errands for them, to picking clients up and dropping them off at the airport.

"I'm sure I have an atypical business plan for Wanda's Waiting," she says. "My goal is to only work a few times a month, at most once or twice a week. I have no plans to grow my business, because then it becomes work." Her financial goal for the business is to generate at least enough income to cover the cost of her long-term care insurance, rather than having to fund it out of her pension. "I hesitated to take out a long-term care policy with the high premiums I have to pay as a diabetic with other health concerns, but darn if I didn't forget to have children, so I'll need support in the final chapters of my life."

Since Wanda started Wanda's Waiting in 2008, it has more than met both her personal and her financial goals. In a good year, the venture generates about $1,000 per month, and even in the worst year it has produced enough income to cover Wanda's long-term care insurance premiums. And on a personal level, the enterprise has succeeded as well. "I'm an extrovert—if you haven't noticed—and this gets me out of the house and about town. It also gives me some joy to know I can succeed outside of my comfort zone. This is like nothing I've ever done before, and it's rewarding to see it succeed." She also points out that since she's free to set her own schedule, it leaves her the flexibility to enjoy her other favorite pastimes, including travel—something Wanda has been doing a lot of since she retired, as a photo of her riding a camel in front of Egypt's Great Pyramid proves.

When I ask Wanda for her best retirement advice for someone like herself, without missing a beat she says, "If you aren't healthy, work to get healthy. And if you are healthy, work to stay that way. You've heard it your whole life—'If you have your health, you have everything'—and by gosh, by golly, it's the truth!"

Wanda is taking her own advice, working hard to lose weight on a reasonable diet ("fifty pounds so far!"), getting more exercise, and trying to manage her own health care more actively—a move that has already helped to greatly reduce the number of prescription medicines she takes.

"My goal is to be in the best shape of my life on the day I die!" she says with a laugh. "I want people at my funeral to say, 'It's so, so sad she's gone, but dang doesn't she look great!' In fact, Jeff, if I happen to pass before you, will you promise me that you'll say that at my funeral? If you do, I'll put in a good word for you (wink) . . . assuming we're both headed to the same place."

CHAPTER 8

I'm Not Retired—I'm Selfishly Employed

The American Dream has never been a single dream, but many different dreams. What's more, from time to time those dreams change for us individually, and even for us as a society. For many, the American Dream includes getting a good education, raising a family, buying a home, and generally living a happy, healthy, and prosperous life.

As discussed earlier, the American Dream or expectations about retirement have been on the move a lot recently, including the trend toward a record number of people now working part-time during their retirement years. Whether out of economic necessity or, more commonly, a desire to remain active—or both—weaving at least a modest amount of paid labor into retirement is a common strategy for those looking to retire the cheapskate way.

While more and more businesses are providing part-time employment opportunities for retirees (see sidebar, pages 249–250), including some that provide access to health care and other valuable benefits, many of my fellow cheapskates and I are combining our retirements with another common version of the American Dream: starting our own businesses. A 2005 poll by Junior Achievement found that almost 70 percent of US teenagers said they wanted to become entrepreneurs during their lifetime, yet in reality only about 10 percent of Americans ever take that plunge.

Ton-tog-an-y. Isn't That Cheyenne for "It's Never Too Late"?

"Every lunch hour, and I mean *every* lunch hour, I thought about it. I had a stack of spiral notebooks hidden in my office, filled with endless noodlings about plans, projections . . . all the numbers. But, you know, I could never make the numbers work." Dan Zeller is telling me about his nearly lifelong dream of starting his own "pet day care" business or even a full-blown kennel and horse boarding operation.

While his love of animals and the idea of being his own boss was daydream fodder throughout most of his thirty-seven-year career as a CPA with various firms in the Chicago area, Dan realized that he'd be lucky to earn even a third of what he was pulling down in his day job if he followed his passion and tried starting the type of business that consumed his lunch-hour thoughts. "I guess that's one of the hazards of being a professional bean counter," he says. "You know too much—or at least *think* too much—about the numbers and what's realistic. With a mortgage and two daughters to put through college, there's no way I could chance it.

"When I first retired, I thought that was that . . . I'd had my career, I'd finished my work." But that's when Dan had an accountant's epiphany: "What I realized was that while it's hard for most people to earn a living doing the things that really turn them on, when it's only a matter of having to earn *at* a living, things look a whole lot different."

Earning *at* a living—having enough financial freedom to pursue your passions as a small business venture of your own, without risking too much or depending too much on any income from it—is what I call the luxury of being "selfishly employed." And, as Dan is learning, once you're officially "retired," the door is wide open for joining the ranks of the selfishly employed.

A few months after Dan retired, a friend who knew of his love of pets asked Dan if he'd mind dog sitting while the couple was away on vacation. "It was such a great experience. My daydreams of doing something like this for a living came flooding back, and I realized that now the numbers had all changed. That's when I started to think of it as 'making *at* a living' . . . starting small, risking nothing but my time, and not worrying about whether I'd ever earn a nickel at it. It was the most refreshing, exciting feeling," Dan says, adding with a quick smile, "but then again, I was an accountant for almost forty years, so I'm easily excited."

With "an investment of absolute zero . . . just my level of risk tolerance," Dan relied on word of mouth and a few flyers posted in businesses around the neighborhood to advertise his pet sitting and pet walking services. "To be honest with you, at first I felt a little silly doing it . . . like a sixty-year old kid starting a lemonade stand. I was thinking I might get a call or two out of it, but that would be about it." Well, in fact, Dan got seven calls, and that was just in the first two days of announcing his selfish employment venture.

Now he has a list of regular clients that keeps him busy to the point where he's no longer adding to it. And there have been a couple of other unexpected perks of Dan's new gig: spending time with his three grandkids, who sometimes help him with "walking duties," and—his wife, Joan, confesses—getting Dan out of the house and out of Joan's hair for a couple of hours most days. In less than a year, Dan's business has grown to the point where he's even looking into the possibility of leasing a small building that formerly housed a pet shop and would be more or less "leash-ready," as he puts it, for a pet day care and boarding facility.

But Dan's not entirely convinced that he wants to take his selfish employment to that next level. He realizes that it would involve at least a modest financial investment risk and might well grow into more of a full-time job than he really wants at this point in his life. "And that's the great, great thing about it; I can decide. I don't *need* to do it (expand or work more hours) to earn a living. I only need to do it if I *want* to do it. As I like to say, 'A bad day walking dogs beats a good day counting beans, every time.'"

"It's Only Work If Somebody Makes You Do It!"

That's a quote from Calvin, costar of the comic strip *Calvin and Hobbes,* by Bill Watterson, but there's a lot of not-so-funny truth to it. Turning a hobby, skill, expertise, or other passion into a cottage industry during retirement—becoming selfishly employed—can be an exciting and rewarding experience. Of course, the rewards may not primarily be financial, but that's okay. Adopt Dan Zeller's perspective and simply view it as earning *at* a living, and who knows what might happen.

When I left my last "real job" as a nonprofit fund-raiser at the age of forty-seven, I wasn't ready, financially or personally, to flat-out retire. That's when I, too, started looking at life and "work" differently. Without a penny of debt and with at least enough savings to keep lentils on the dinner table, I realized that while my wife and I couldn't afford to fully retire at that point, we could at least afford the luxury of becoming selfishly employed.

As a lifelong teacher, my wife loves being in front of a class and mentoring students. But she'd grown tired of the overloaded class schedules and administrative hassles that come with most full-time teaching positions. So, for Denise, selfish employment has meant still teaching, but teaching more on her own terms: part-time, selecting just the courses she wants to teach, and occasionally designing and offering new courses of her own. As I've often told her since she made that career shift, "You smile a lot more these days."

Unlike Denise, I was far less certain about what form my selfish employment would take. I don't suffer for lack of hobbies and other interests, and that was part of the problem in deciding which direction to pursue. In fact, I took a full year just to explore multiple directions simultaneously. I dabbled at buying and selling antiques and other unique artifacts through a local consignment shop; I tried to parlay my love of gardening and working outdoors into some project work for neighbors; I even became "the Bonsai Guy" for a while, attempting to turn my interest in raising bonsai plants into a cottage industry. Unfortunately—but quite fittingly—that last business venture was, as I said at the time, "too small and slow growing to ever really take root."

But it was also during that year that I rediscovered and began to once again indulge my love of writing. Not the kind of business writing that I'd done almost every day of my twenty-four-year career in the nonprofit sector, but the more creative type of writing that had been a passion of mine in high school and college, before my nose met the grindstone and I forgot all about it.

At first it seemed crazy that at nearly fifty I could launch an entirely new career as a writer and author. But like Dan, I was both comforted and energized in knowing that I didn't *need* to earn a full-time living doing it. That freedom to fail, or to set different measures for my success, or to change my mind or direction entirely at any time—none of that I'd ever had the luxury of experiencing before in my life. And, frankly, it enthused me even more than triple-coupon day at the Safeway store.

That was three books ago, and I can tell you that at this point I don't think I'll ever fully retire. I'm having too much fun being selfishly employed.

Cheapskate Retirement Principle #15

One path to early retirement is to keep working as long as you possibly can . . . BUT, also as early as you possibly can, transform that work into a *selfish employment* venture. Remember, it's only work if somebody makes you do it.

Some Selfish Employment Considerations

Keeping that Cheapskate Retirement Principle in mind, there are some important things to consider before diving into a selfish employment venture.

First, remember, by "selfishly employed" I'm not suggesting that you go out and buy an existing business, or buy into a franchise plan, or start a full-time traditional business with staff, offices, and high overhead. Nor am I talking about getting a part-time job working for someone else, although there's nothing wrong with any of those options.

Rather, by "selfish employment" I mean creating a part-time employment opportunity simply for one person, yourself. And the good news is, if you do, you're a shoe-in for "Employee of the Month" twelve times a year! **You** and your skills and services are the primary product you're marketing. Ideally it will be a venture that requires little if any investment of capital, and it will most likely be one that is based out of your home.

Here are six key things to consider in setting up your selfish employment venture:

1. **Minimal Investment/Risk.** As I've said before, you *don't* need to always spend money to make money, particularly when you're selfishly employed. After all, your inventory is primarily you, your time, and your skills. Like Dan's pet care service, my writing business cost me absolutely nothing to start, since I already owned a computer, a desk, five packets of Post-it Notes, a Swingline stapler, a large supply of Rolaids, and the few other essential tools of the writing trade. Sure, some selfish employment ventures might require an up-front or eventual investment of funds, but of the fifty part-time business ideas listed below, I can't imagine that any would require an initial

investment of more than, say, $1,000 (e.g., equipment, training, etc.), and most could be launched for nothing at all. My advice is to think long and hard before launching any selfish employment venture that requires you to risk more than a grand up front.

2. **Social Security Implications.** It's important to understand that earning wage income while drawing Social Security benefits *can* decrease or even eliminate those benefits. But it's a little complicated. If, for example, you begin drawing Social Security benefits before your "full retirement age" (see Chapter 5), under 2012 rules you can earn up to $14,640 in annual wage income without any reduction in benefits; for every $2 in wages you earn above that amount, your Social Security benefits are reduced by $1. Once you reach full retirement age, you can earn $38,880 a year and not lose any benefits (per 2012 rules), but your Social Security benefit will be reduced by $1 for every $3 earned above $38,880. So there's a bit of a disincentive to earn too much through your part-time employment, particularly if you decide to start drawing Social Security benefits before your full retirement age. The earning limits usually change annually, and the rules are fairly complex, but Social Security Administration Publication 05-10069 *How Work Affects Your Benefits* (www.ssa.gov/pubs/10069 .html#a0=6), explains all the details. For the selfishly employed, it's also important to note that if you work for

yourself while drawing Social Security, only *net* earnings from your work (i.e., amounts left after allowable expenses) are counted as part of those earning limits.

☞ *You might need a Cheapskate Intervention if you think foreign ATM fees are actually reward points you're earning that can be redeemed for international travel.*

3. **Tax and Legal Issues.** Every type of business venture has its own set of legal and tax issues that need to be carefully researched and managed. Of the fifty ideas for becoming selfishly employed listed on pages 232–248, most raise minimal concerns in terms of personal liability, local zoning, licensing, and so forth, although some do, so do your homework and consult a qualified attorney. You should also become familiar with industry standards pertinent to your chosen field and any certifications or training required to meet those standards. In some cases, it may make sense to incorporate your business, perhaps forming a limited liability company (LLC), although in many cases you can function just fine as an unincorporated "sole proprietorship." Also on the positive side, operating a small business—particularly one based out of your home—can offer attractive tax advantages (see IRS Publications 334, *Tax Guide for Small Business*, and 587, *Business Use of Your Home*, and talk with a tax

professional about your individual situation). In addition to seeking professional legal and tax advice, I have found the Nolo (www.Nolo.com) series of books and other resources they provide for small businesses to be very helpful.

4. **Turning an Enjoyable Hobby into an Unenjoyable Job.** This is a common problem, particularly if you're attempting to turn a longtime hobby, craft, or other enjoyable pastime into a selfish employment venture. Miser Adviser Margaret Fowl loved making costume jewelry for friends and family before she retired, so it seemed like a perfect chance for her to build a little side business and generate some additional income when she retired at age sixty-two. Between word of mouth, craft fairs, and interest from consignment shops in carrying her jewelry, Margaret's business quickly took off. "One day I was sitting at my worktable, surrounded by beads and chains and tools, and I thought, 'This isn't fun anymore. I feel like a machine,'" she says. Fortunately, being selfishly employed, Margaret finished up her outstanding orders and then promptly fired herself and closed up shop. After a short respite, she's once again enjoying her hobby by going back to making jewelery just for friends and family ("and occasional special orders, if the price is right"). She also now teaches a few jewelry-making classes through her church and other local organizations, which allows her to share her love of

the craft with others without being transformed into a jewelry-making robot.

5. **Planning for Success More Than Failure.** It sounds odd, but when you go into a selfish employment venture knowing that nothing awful is going to happen if you fail, you don't have to waste a second thinking about failure. But you should spend some time thinking about and planning for how you might manage just the opposite: success. As Dan has already found in his pet care business and as I've bumped up against in my own selfish employment, it's very possible that things will trend positive, your venture will grow, and opportunities will present themselves for your part-time gig to become full-time or even *more* than full-time. Managing growth, keeping expectations in check (yours as well as your clients' and other partners'), and having a plan in mind should your own success overtake you are all things to consider sooner rather than later.

6. **Setting Boundaries.** As rewarding as selfish employment can be—and as important as it can be as part of a strategy for early retirement—like so many things in life, *balance* is the key. If you're not careful, your selfish employment venture can take over everything from too much of your time to too much of your house, more so than you ever imagined. Keep that part of your life separate: separate in terms of your schedule, your finances,

and your physical space. Set aside specific times when you work on your venture, as well as a specific location (e.g., home office, workshop, spare bedroom, etc.) where you work from. And most of all, while you may very well find your selfish employment venture to be one of the most enjoyable components of your "retirement," remember that it's *only one component*; take great care to never lose sight of all the other important things in your life-after-work.

50 No-Risk/Low-Risk Opportunities to Become Selfishly Employed

— — — — — — — —

Having trouble coming up with a selfish employment venture of your own? Try these on for size:

Consultant Of course this is perhaps the most common form of selfish employment for retirees, simply tapping the expertise and contacts you developed in your former career and selling your time—as much or as little of it as you like—by the hour. The Association of Professional Consultants (www.consultapc.org), the Association of Consultants to Nonprofits (www.acnconsult.org), and the Institute of Management Consultants USA (www .imcusa.org) are all professional nonprofit groups that can help you get started.

Professional organizer   Helping busy people, businesses, and plain old slobs organize everything from their closets and paperwork to decluttering their entire lives is a growing field. Check out the National Association of Professional Organizers (www.napo.net).

Office plant care   If you have a green thumb and live in an urban/suburban area, reach out to large businesses and office complexes to see if you can provide weekly care for their office plants. The up-front investment is little more than a watering can and some Miracle-Gro, and it's possible to expand into furnishing offices with plants as well, either on a resale or a "rental" basis.

Website designer   With more than 350 MILLION websites now on the Internet, there are plenty of opportunities to earn a few bucks as a freelance website designer if you have the skills. One easy way to promote your services is through the vast and ever-growing network of online job sites for freelancers—and not just for website design freelancers, but freelancers of all kinds. You post info about your skills and services, and folks looking to outsource projects to freelancers post their job openings. Sites like www.allfreelance.com and www.modernfreelance.com act as clearinghouses, providing directories of other sites and job boards as well as general information on freelancing.

Artist   Painting, sculpting, pottery, you name it. If you're artistically inclined, this is the time in your life to start calling yourself "an artist" whenever anyone asks you what you do. And why not? Declaring yourself selfishly employed as an artist is perfectly legitimate even if you never sell a single piece, since that's not a prerequisite for being selfishly employed. The up-front investment in art supplies, tools, and any desired training is usually minimal. In addition to marketing your work through traditional galleries, gift shops, and arts/crafts shows, websites like www.Etsy.com specialize in helping individual artists and craftspeople sell their wares over the Internet to a worldwide market.

Cake decorator With the average cost of a wedding cake now at about $600 (per the Bridal Association of America) and tricked-out, customized cakes all the rage these days, it may be time to fill up your pastry bag and hang out your shingle (or sheet cake?). Check with your local community college and vocational schools for courses in cake decorating.

Power washer There's something about guys and hoses, and a retired friend of mine has built a nice part-time income *stream* around a pressure washer he bought used for under $200. Hosing down decks, driveways, houses, and the like can be a low-risk selfish employment venture with a minimal up-front investment, so you're not likely to get *hosed* if you give it a try and don't like it.

Fitness instructor/personal trainer The demand for "more mature" fitness instructors and personal trainers—folks who actually understand how we can and *can't* bend any-more—is increasing as we baby boomers age. There are many organizations and commercial businesses that offer certifications in these fields, including the gold-standard National Academy of Sports Medicine (www.nasm.org), but research others carefully to make sure they provide adequate training and the credibility for what you want to do.

Editorial services With the growing popularity of e-books and self-publishing, freelance editors and proofreaders—and even fact checkers and indexers—are in demand. The Editorial Freelancers Association (www.the-efa.org) can help you get started.

Personal chef By preparing meals for busy people in their own homes or using their kitchens to cater events they host, you can often avoid some of the regulations and requirements that apply to commercial catering and other food services operations. Check out the US Personal Chef Association (www.uspca.com).

Media escort I've given serious thought to entering this little-known, high-paying field myself. When celebrities and authors (although apparently not cheapskate authors . . . we ride our bicycles instead) do a publicity/book tour, often a freelance "media escort" is hired in each metro area they visit simply to drive them around and make sure they get to where they need to be and stay happy. The fee can easily be $500 to $1,000 per day or more. Every city usually has a couple of companies that provide media escorts, so check in with them and let them know of your availability or set up your own media escort service.

Private tutor   For better or worse, hanging out your shingle as a "private tutor" in the United States is typically subject to no educational or other prerequisites whatsoever, regardless of field. It's a "let the tutored beware" system, so if you're able to successfully teach a pupil to his or her—or commonly the parents'—satisfaction, that's all that matters. The easiest way to get started is to reach out to full-time teachers and principals in your area and let them know that you're available for private tutoring in their field. Also try contacting homeschoolers in your community, and consider specializing in helping students prepare to take specialized exams, such as the GED, SAT, and GRE.

Party/wedding planner   This is big business these days with so many people too busy to organize their own personal events. Of course, there is an association (actually a number of them) for professional wedding planners (see www.aacwp.org), but I suppose it's also possible to just watch the Jennifer Lopez movie by the same name and start out that way, growing your business through word of mouth.

☞ *You might need a Cheapskate Intervention if you sent your bank account information to the barrister representing the exiled Prince of Burundi so that he can wire you the $3.2 billion he promised you in his e-mail message.*

Corporate trainer/coach In this branch of corporate consulting, the focus is on stand-up training for staff and one-on-one coaching for staff members who can benefit from your experience and knowledge. If you have a successful background in sales, sales coaches are particularly in demand these days to mentor those with less experience and few client contacts. As with general consulting, the place to start is with the business network from your previous full-time career.

Disc jockey Keeping the music flowing at wedding receptions, parties, and other social events pays well and can help you keep your groove on. Investing in your own commercial-quality sound equipment up front can be pricey, but it's also possible to rent it for individual gigs, at least until you see if you've got what it takes to be a pancake turner.

Hit man *See* Disc jockey, *above.*

Blogger Starting a website or a blog online is easy, inexpensive (or even free), and can be a fun creative outlet. It's also possible to generate income through your website/blog by allowing advertising on the site, charging for content, or even asking readers for voluntary contributions if they like what you write. In general, the blogs/websites with the greatest financial return are ones that focus on a specific topic of interest to both readers and advertisers (e.g., personal finance, health/fitness, homemaking, specific hobbies, etc.). The website www.problogger.net is a great resource for those with an interest. Also, if you have specific expertise to share, it may be possible to be paid by an existing website related to that field to simply write a blog that will be published on that site.

Personal concierge/assistant Remember Wanda Adams, my Miser Adviser Emerita, who retired from teaching in the Dayton area and created "Wanda's Waiting" (www .WandasWaiting.com)? It's a great idea for a selfish employment venture. She'll do everything from waiting in your home for a repairman while you're at work, to driving you to and from the airport, to even taking you shopping.

Crafter Other than turning a former profession into a consulting practice, turning a craft or other hobby into a cottage industry is probably the most common form of selfish employment. But heed the advice of Margaret Fowl, the jewelry maker, and take it slow. Also don't overinvest in supplies and inventory up front, as the market for gold leaf murals of Elvis may not be quite as brisk as you think it is.

Genealogist/personal historian/biographer If you enjoy researching and documenting your own family history, you should consider it as a possibility for selfish employment. As you probably know from researching your own family history, it can be time-consuming and requires skill, so it's the kind of service some people will gladly outsource. The Board for Certification of Genealogists (www.bcg certification.org) is one of the organizations that provides related training and certification. And if you're a strong writer, combining your researching and writing skills in order to produce personal histories or formal biographies for clients can be particularly lucrative.

Bicycle mechanic I earned my way through college by repairing bicycles out of my parents' garage. If you're at all mechanically inclined and don't mind getting a little greasy, the skills are fairly easy to master. And, unlike with auto mechanics, the up-front investment in tools and other equipment is minimal. Classes are taught at some community colleges, or you can pick up the skills by apprenticing at a bike shop.

Life coach I've never understood why every "life coach" I've ever met seems to be twenty-four years old and still living with his parents. What the heck does he have to teach anybody about life? On the other hand, older folks—particularly those who have learned the secrets of retiring better, earlier, and happier—have a wealth of life knowledge and experiences to share. Websites like www.becomealifecoachnow.com and www.mylifecoach .com abound and explain what's involved.

Musician Maybe it's time to get your old garage band back together and have an all-night jam session (well, or at least until, say, 9:30 or so) and try to land a few paying gigs. After all, it's *your* garage now, not your parents', so who cares about the noise? Not surprisingly, some oldie-but-never-very-goodie garage bands are reuniting as their members retire from the rat race, and some of them are pretty popular. Check out the book *The Indie Band*

Survival Guide, by Randy Chertkow and Jason Feehan, for tips on making a comeback . . . even if you never had a heyday in the first place.

Pet care services Borrow the business model from "Dan the former bean counter," and start out small by advertising your availability for pet sitting and walking services through word of mouth and flyers posted around the neighborhood. Websites like www.mypetbusiness.com offer advice and resources for taking it to the next level if you want an even bigger dose of puppy love.

Public speaker If you have something worthwhile to say (who doesn't?) and enjoy speaking in front of groups, there are all types of public speaking opportunities available, dealing with every subject matter imaginable. Compensation ranges from a free lunch to many thousands of dollars for delivering a single speech, depending on the group and your experience. Hone your speaking skills—and have some fun—by joining Toastmasters International (www.toastmasters.org) and check out professional organizations like the National Speakers Association (www.nsaspeaker.org).

Gardening/landscaper Turn your green thumb into the kind of green you can spend, and get some exercise at the same time. If you have the tools to care for your own yard and garden, you have everything you need to start a selfishly employed venture offering to do the same for others.

Private tour guide If you live in an area frequented by tourists, let your local visitor's bureau and chamber of commerce know that you're available to provide private tours of area attractions to groups and individuals. If you want to get really serious about it, check out the National Federation of Tour Guide Associations (www.nftga.com).

Meeting/event planner Midsize and smaller businesses and nonprofit organizations often outsource their meeting and event planning needs to freelancers. Being organized, able to multitask, and able to get along with a wide range of personalities are among the essential skills. If you know of businesses or other organizations that have an annual conference, trade show, or other type of special event, contact them directly with your sales pitch.

Porn star Okay, maybe not. But I'm pretty sure if Danny DeVito ever agrees to do a sex scene in a movie and needs a body double, I've got the role.

Personal shopper Who could be more qualified than a cheapskate to shop smartly for people who are too busy to do it themselves? In fact, I've often thought that I could make a handsome part-time income by grocery shopping for other people in exchange for being able to keep the amounts I saved them through couponing and other smart-shopping tricks. Most personal shoppers, though, are paid by the hour (plus mileage), but sometimes they do get a "bonus" based on how much they save a client when they negotiate on the purchase of major-ticket items like a new car. Many personal shoppers specialize in interior design or high-fashion apparel and prefer to be called "image consultants"; the website www.aici.org is a resource for image consultants.

Handyman How many times have you wished you had a good old-fashioned handyman (or handywoman) on speed dial? Everyone is a specialist these days—and charges like one—when sometimes all you really need is someone with the right tools and enough general knowledge for the occasional odd job around the house. Go back-to-the-future and hang out your shingle as a trusty handyman in the tradition of George Utley from the old *Newhart* show.

Party clown No, not the drunk kind with a lampshade on his head, but the kind that gets paid to entertain at kids' birthday parties and other events. Now you can even get clown training online—including the skinny on turning it into a business—at the Academy of Performing Arts in Clowning (www.clownschool.net).

Seamstress If you love to sew, look no further for your selfish employment business opportunity. Repairing, tailoring, or even creating a new clothing line of your own is a perfect home-based, low-investment venture. Promote your services through flyers at local Laundromats and dry cleaners. Or consider starting a "refashioning" business, remodeling old clothing into new, like Miser Adviser Jenny Jo Allen, of Port Townsend, Washington (www.jennyjoclothing.com).

Floral designer With custom floral arrangements easily costing $50 to $100 or more, there's a lot of cash in those carnation creations. Many community colleges and vocational schools offer courses in floral design, and—depending on the size of your operation—buying cut flowers in bulk at membership warehouse stores like Costco and Sam's Club may be the only supplier you need. Contact wedding planners, churches, and even funeral homes to let them know of your services.

Reseller of stuff Buying and reselling other people's stuff—or helping them to sell it—is a popular cottage industry these days. From old-school business models like establishing a permanent "garage sale" at your house (local codes permitting), to the resale craze on sites like eBay and Craigslist, apparently there are as many willing buyers as there are storage units filled with unwanted stuff. Another approach is to offer to help other people sell their items online or by organizing a garage/estate sale for them; payment for these types of services can be based on an hourly or flat fee and/or commissions on actual sales.

Car detailing Doesn't sound like fun to me, but I know a lot of guys who get a kick—and make decent money—by primping and polishing other people's rides, inside and out. The up-front investment in equipment is minimal, and the service is often provided at people's homes or places of business.

Stand-up comedian "A lawyer, a doctor, and a cheapskate arrive in heaven at the same time . . . " I've found that one of the great things about growing older is that you become inoculated against public embarrassment—at my age, I just don't care what other people think anymore. How-to courses in stand-up comedy are common in major metro areas; there are even some online courses. Or just hang out at comedy clubs, listen to other people's acts, and then get your nerve up on open mike night.

Athletic coach/official   Coaching or officiating at the amateur sports level can be both personally and financially rewarding. Whether it's being an umpire, a referee, a scorekeeper, or a coach, check with youth and amateur leagues in your area for available positions. Seasonal coaching positions at schools often pay $3,000 to $5,000, and officials are usually compensated by the game, typically in the $30 to $50 range per gig. Different certifications and training may be required; the National Association of Sports Officials (www.naso.org) is a good place to find out more.

☞ *You might need a Cheapskate Intervention if you think a 401(k) is a brand of stain remover.*

House sitter   Keeping an eye on people's homes while they're away—either by temporarily moving in or just by making the rounds every day or so—is an easy way to make some extra money. Get your references in order and rely on word of mouth to get started, and once you get a reputation as a dependable caretaker, generating regular business shouldn't be difficult.

Dumpster diver   Scavenging for items that can be resold or that you can use yourself saves both money and the earth's resources. Check out the classic book on the subject, *The Scavengers' Manifesto*, by Anneli Rufus and Kristan Lawson.

Babysitter/nanny   Of course if you have grandkids, you may already have your fill of kiddie-care responsibilities. But spending time around children—particularly when they're not your own—can keep you young and generate some decent income. And an increasing number of retirees are accepting nanny and other domestic positions with families that sometimes carry with them the benefit of complimentary room and board—talk about nice perks.

Author/freelance writer   Once upon a time I saw a survey that showed that 80 percent of Americans say they want to write a book during their lifetime. Again, it's never too late, particularly now with e-book technology making it possible for anyone to self-publish a book with little or no up-front investment. I can't guarantee you'll make any money from it, but unlike with old-fashioned "vanity presses," you at least shouldn't *lose* any money if you're smart about it. Check out *Writer's Digest* magazine (www.WritersDigest.com) for information on launching your selfish employment career as a freelance writer or author, but just stay away from my cheapskate genre turf, please.

Street performer   Think outside the mime in the box.

Check out these popular—and well-compensated—street performers in Barcelona, Spain, at www.youtube .com/watch?v=y79hLcP41U8. Definitely an idea worth importing.

Chimney sweep "Chim chimney, chim chimney, chim chim I'm cheap . . . " Or something like that. It's much more of a science and safety concern than simply dancing around on rooftops in a top hat, but you can find the details on how to get involved in this sooty profession at www.chimneysweepers.com.

Calligrapher With my poor penmanship, this isn't an option (I once had my handwriting analyzed, and the expert analyst asked whether or not it was in English!), but there's always a demand for talented scribes. Calligraphers commonly charge $2 to $5 each to address envelopes for wedding invitations, for example, with longer jobs like certificates of recognition and official proclamations priced by the character. Art schools and private calligraphers often offer lessons locally, and you can even learn the craft online or—most fittingly—through "correspondence" courses as well (www.calligraphyonline.org).

Psychic/palm reader I agree; they're fakes. But if you have a client foolish enough to pay you to predict their future, I'm pretty sure you'll be foretelling the truth if you say to them, "I see you wasting even more money in the future."

Photographer/videographer If you're skilled with a camera, market your services through wedding and party planners, to corporate and fundraising events, and even to local newspapers and online news sites that often buy images and video footage from freelancers.

Home inspector/eco-consultant Inspecting homes as part of the real estate buying/selling process and providing "preventive checkups" is a great part-time opportunity for the selfishly employed. It does require training and certification, which varies by state; you can find individual state requirements at www.hometraining .com, and you can get additional information from the American Society of Home Inspectors (www.ashi.org). Also, consulting with homeowners specifically about environmental and energy efficiency issues pertaining to their residences is a growing field; see www.greenpages .org for more info on home eco-consulting.

Mystery shopper It's with great trepidation that I even mention this as a possibility for selfish employment, since there are far more scams out there advertising opportunities to be "paid to shop" as a "mystery shopper" than there are legitimate part-time employment opportunities. BUT there are some legitimate mystery shopper gigs to be had—these are typically one-off assignments to patronize a particular retailer, restaurant, or so on, and report back on your shopping experience or level of customer satisfaction. Mystery shoppers are normally reimbursed for what they spend and get to keep the booty, and some are occasionally paid a fee as well. But beware of all the scams advertising "Mystery Shoppers Wanted" and asking you to pay *them* money for registration, info packets, and so on. Becoming a mystery shopper for a legitimate company doesn't cost you anything; register and find out more through the Mystery Shopping Providers Association (www.mysteryshop.org).

Professional cheapskate   Not that I'm looking to encourage any competition, but I'm amazed at how many people with a spending problem contact me to ask if I provide "private consulting services" to help them get their spending under control. Of course, in my opinion, if you're looking to *pay* someone to help you spend less, you're likely a lost cause. But, who knows, it may be a viable selfish employment opportunity for some of my enterprising cheapskate friends.

Cheapskate Retirement Principle #16

Whether by joining the ranks of the selfishly employed or by simply landing a part-time job working for someone else, if you're physically able, cheapskates say the smart thing to do is to work at least enough during your initial retirement years to earn the maximum amount allowable without reducing your Social Security

benefit. It will keep you active and involved, and, when coupled with Social Security, it *could* be enough to cover at least your essential expenses.

BUT I DON'T WANT TO BE MY OWN BOSS! FINDING THE BEST PART-TIME JOBS FOR RETIREES

Fair enough, "selfish employment" isn't for everyone. But there is a lot to be said for continuing to bring in some part-time income at least during the front end of your retirement years, per Cheapskate Retirement Principle #16.

Who's hiring and what they're offering (in terms of both pay and other benefits) of course changes constantly. A number of websites and publications, including www.AARP.org, www.smartmoney.com, and www.careerbuilder.com often run updated listings on their picks for best part-time employers. Some nationwide companies that consistently rank high on those lists include Barnes & Noble, FedEx, JCPenney, JPMorgan Chase, Costco (now there's a part-time dream job for a cheapskate!), Lands' End, Lowe's, Nordstrom, Publix, REI (Recreational Equipment Inc.), Starbucks, Target, Trader Joe's, U-Haul, UPS, Wegmans, Whole Foods Market, and YMCA.

Part-time positions with these companies aren't just for retirees, of course, and they usually make the best-of-the-best lists because they often offer some provisions for part-time employees to tap into benefit plans normally reserved for full-time workers. Be forewarned, though, that the availability of benefits varies for part-time employees and commonly involves meeting a number of requirements, such as working a minimum number of hours per week or meeting length-of-service requirements.

And here's a part-time employer you might not think about: the government. Many federal government agencies offer part-time and seasonal jobs, as do some state, county, and municipal governments. The benefits for governmental part-timers are often better than those in the private sector, and age discrimination in hiring is likely to be less of an issue. Check out www.usajobs.gov to get started.

DAVE AND LINDA ALLEN

Cruising Through a Cheapskate Retirement

"Come in, *Irish Melody*. Do you copy? Bad news to report. Over."

Obviously, words like those could never be good to hear. Particularly when you're receiving them via a ham radio while bobbing around in a thirty-eight-foot sailboat off the coast of the Marquesas Islands in the South Pacific; and especially, I suppose, if you're receiving them from the financial consigliere you've appointed to manage your money matters while you spend a decade—or two—sailing the high seas during your retirement.

Given the source of the radio communications, I guess the good news was that the bad news wasn't likely to be a warning of an impending typhoon.

But Dave and Linda Allen still braced for the worst when the crackling message came over the radio from Ed Fox. Five years earlier, when the Allens retired in their mid-fifties and set sail to explore the Pacific on a semipermanent basis, they'd left their trusted and financially savvy friend Ed in charge of their finances back in the United States. Ed paid their bills, transferred funds as needed, and generally oversaw the Allens' affairs while they were at sea.

However, since the start of their adventure, Ed had openly expressed his concerns about whether the Allens were actually in a strong enough financial position to retire and travel the world while still relatively young.

"Copy that, Ed," Dave nervously responded over the radio. "What's the problem? Over."

After what seemed like an interminable pause, Ed's voice again crackled over the airwaves.

"Although I never thought it was possible, having seen how well the two of you have done living on your limited retirement income and how much fun you're having, you've convinced me that I can afford to retire, too. Marge and I have our bags all packed, and we're taking off to see the world ourselves. Sorry, I'll no longer be able to administer your finances while you're cruising. Love to you both. Over and out."

The Allens spent most of the rest of the night laughing and reveling in their friend's good news. (Just for the record, Ed did help the Allens find a new, younger financial manager before he and Marge hit the road, one who is still balancing their books twelve years later.)

In Chapter 2 I mentioned a fascinating study sponsored by SunAmerica that, among other things, identified a number of distinct types of retirees based on how they view retirement and plan for it. One of the categories of retirees was labeled "Ageless Explorers." It could just as well have been called "Linda and Dave Allens."

According to the study, these are the folks who are at the forefront of the trend toward radically redefining what retirement means. Ageless Explorers don't view retirement as a period of winding down in life—just the opposite. For Ageless Explorers, retirement is the time in life to really ramp things up, reinvent yourself as you'd like, and live out the biggest dreams you've ever dared to dream. Even if it means taking some risks—financial and otherwise—to make it happen.

Dave Allen, now seventy-two, is tall and rail-thin, with a beard that would be the envy of any Amish grandpa. He could pass for a graying Abe Lincoln—or maybe Abe's second cousin—and even has the same thoughtful, soft-spoken style that I've always imagined as characteristic of Honest Abe. Dave has a dry, somewhat understated sense of humor. But when you put a fiddle in his hands, everything about him—and everyone in the room—lights up like the strands of colorful twinkle lights he and Linda sometimes string from the masts of *Irish Melody*.

Linda, seventy-one, is also tall and thin, with long hair and pretty features. It's clear that the couple is more fit than lots of people half their age, and they probably have less body fat between the two of them than most individual

Americans carry around with them every day. Linda has intense, piercing brown eyes and a chortling laugh that naturally puts people at ease.

It strikes me that the Allens are the kind of people whom *anyone* would instantly feel comfortable being around, even if they didn't share a common language. And that has come in handy time and again in their world travels, when, in fact, they've often found themselves in situations where language barriers have made nonverbal communication the most important form of communication.

The Allens have always had a love of travel and adventure and did as much of both as they could afford even as they raised their two children, Jenny and Bob, and Dave worked as a civil engineer at the Sonoma County Water Agency in Santa Rosa, California. The couple met in junior college in 1958 and married six years later. Linda taught second grade while Dave completed his engineering degree at Sacramento State.

"Even at that time, when I was the only one working and not making much money as a new teacher, it always seemed like we had more money than we really needed," Linda recalls of those early years when the couple rented a small walk-up apartment and lived a simple but comfortable life. "I remember other teachers at my school lining up on payday to get their paychecks so they could rush to the bank and deposit them to cover the checks they'd already written. Sometimes I'd even forget it was payday." In fact, even during that period, the Allens were able to scrape together enough extra money to spend nine weeks in Europe one summer, staying in hostels and traveling on the cheap.

In 1970 the couple moved to Santa Rosa and bought a fifties-era ranch-style home on a one-acre lot, replete with fruit trees, outdoor living spaces, a small pool, and even a stream running through the property. Not bad for the $26,500 they paid for it. Forty-plus years later, the Allens still call that same *forever house* their home, renting it out during periods when they were traveling and now having returned there on a more or less full-time basis. "We feel so fortunate to already be living in a place where so many people choose to relocate once they retire. It's like we bought our retirement house first, and just stayed there."

The Allens happily settled into Santa Rosa and raised their two children. For the most part Linda was a stay-at-home mom, other than some occasional substitute teaching, and Dave continued working for Sonoma County. They made it a point to teach their children about money—and specifically how to spend it wisely—from a very young age. "We always gave our kids a small allowance and put them in charge of what they did with it," Dave recalls. Eventually they entrusted their children with their own clothing allowance as well, empowering them to spend it however they saw fit. "It made them really smart consumers at a young age," Linda says. Their daughter, Jenny, for example, discovered early on that she could afford a lot more fun clothing if she shopped at thrift stores rather than department stores or bought the latest designer fashions.

Dave was making a relatively good salary with the county, and paying into a pension plan as well. They managed to set aside a college fund for both of their children, eventually paying for their son, Bob, to receive his mechanical engineering degree at Sacramento State. Jenny used a portion of her college fund to study at a junior college for a time before deciding that, with her creative inclinations, she was more interested in starting a small business of her own, which Dave and Linda agreed to support with the balance in her college fund.

The Allens' decision to officially retire and hit the high seas was, to a great extent, almost unplanned. In 1993, the county was looking to trim costs and offered Dave a chance to work fewer hours but still receive full benefits. He could work a four-day week and still make about $50,000 a year—more than enough for the Allens to live on—so he jumped at the chance. "I got used to three-day weekends real fast," Dave says with a little laugh, and he quickly wanted even more free time.

The couple began talking about all the traveling they still wanted to do. Dave began toying with the idea of taking a leave of absence from his job. They checked into the possibility of signing on with the Peace Corps or Habitat for Humanity, but both organizations required multiyear commitments, well beyond what Dave could have arranged as a leave of absence.

Then in 1995, when Dave was fifty-five, his sister and her husband contacted the Allens with a proposition: they wanted to take off again in their sailboat, and if the Allens were willing to help get it in seaworthy condition, the four of them could spend a year cruising the Pacific along the coast of California and Mexico.

"At first we thought that there was no way we could afford to have Dave retire and take off on an adventure like that," Linda says. "But that's when we really started sharpening our pencils," Dave adds, as if almost finishing her sentence. As they're telling me this, I'm thinking to myself, *And that's why they are Ageless Explorers.*

So they decide to take the plunge, Dave retires from the county, and the Allens begin to learn a whole lot about sailing and sailboats, things they'd had only limited experience with prior to that point. But Dave comes from a long line of family members who pride themselves on being able to repair anything (and his degree in engineering doesn't hurt either), so before long the ship was ready to sail.

I'm surprised to learn that when the Allens set sail with Dave's sister and brother-in-law, Dave himself was quite certain he wouldn't like "the cruising lifestyle," as it's called. "I thought it would get boring pretty fast," he recalls. But it wasn't long into that first voyage that the Allens were hooked. The only problem was, their sailing partners—the owners of the boat—were winding down from their sailing years.

However, the Allens were just getting started. Returning to Santa Rosa, they again sharpened their pencils, and— after finding a fifteen-year-old Canadian-built sailboat on the market that met their needs—decided to refinance their home in order to generate the $65,000 they needed to buy the boat they rechristened *Irish Melody*. "We were confident that we could rent out our house while we cruised and that would cover the new mortgage payment," Dave says.

When the couple first set sail in 1996 on *Irish Melody*, they expected that their adventure might last five years or less. "The only thing we agreed on was that when the time came that it wasn't fun anymore, we'd sell the boat and do something else," Linda recalls. At first, the Allens spent most of the "cruising season" (a seven-month period, beginning in November in the South Pacific and April in the north) each year sailing off the Pacific coast of Mexico and California, returning to their home in Santa Rosa during the off-season to visit friends and family. When they returned to Santa Rosa, they'd stay in a small RV they had parked on their property, since the house itself was being rented out.

By 2001, the Allens, then in their sixties, had set their eyes on a faraway new horizon, sailing across the breadth of the Pacific from Mexico to French Polynesia in a twenty-five-day passage. In coming years, they would explore that part of the globe pretty thoroughly, visiting Australia, Tahiti, Fiji, Tonga, Bora-Bora, Palau, Micronesia, the Philippines, the Marshall Islands, and countless other ports of call along the way. Most years, they still continued to fly home to California in the off-season, journeys that added considerably to their annual expenses. While at sea, the living was cheap and easy; they estimate they spent about $2,000 per month on food, fuel, dockage, minor repairs, and other provisions.

That was an amount the Allens could cover with their Social Security benefits alone, without tapping into Dave's pension.

It wasn't until nearly ten years later, while exploring the Marshall Islands and encountering some difficult winds, that Dave turned to Linda and asked her if she was still having fun. That began a discussion about selling the boat, and after a final 3,500 miles of heavenly downwind sailing through the beautiful tropical islands of Micronesia, they knew it was time to let someone else enjoy *Irish Melody.* "So, we decided that sixteen good years of cruising was sufficient and it was time to do something else with the rest of our lives," Linda says.

But what do a couple of septuagenarians do for an encore after returning from more than a decade and half at sea? Well, if you're Ageless Explorers, you don't head for the nearest rocking chair.

Having done it myself, I know that bicycling across the entire United States is tough, even for a young man in his prime riding a state-of-the-art bicycle. But when Dave climbed on his bicycle in Kansas City in 2010 to complete the second half of a cross-country bicycle trip he'd started in 1986 and always wanted to finish, his then 70+-year-old legs weren't his biggest challenge. You see, Dave insisted on completing most of the remaining 1,800-mile-ride to the East Coast on the same bike he'd used originally, an old-fashioned single-speed "high wheeler" built in 1888. *Can't this guy ever take the path at least a little bit more traveled?*

With Linda driving their RV, where they spent the nights,

as one might guess their journey was filled with adventures as well as misadventures. In the Midwest, Dave crashed while going about 30 miles an hour down a hill ("no broken bones, but six stitches and skin lost in twelve places"). Five days later, in Kentucky, he was attacked by three pit bulls, resulting in bites on both legs. (Dave's legs, that is: "I never did manage to bite them back.")

Since returning from that adventure, the Allens have been settling down a bit, except for little side trips like their recent jaunts to Canada, Mexico, China, Singapore, Vietnam, and Korea. They're currently working to partition their house in Santa Rosa so that they'll have a small unit they can continue to rent out in order to generate some additional income. They insist they are taking it a little easier, spending time with their grandkids, getting involved in community activities, and pursuing a wide range of hobbies and other interests.

"Eventually, we plan to let a caregiver live in the rental unit as part of a package to help us as we become less able and slow down," Linda says. That sounds like a reasonable plan. But then I think to myself, *Yeah, like Dave and Linda Allen are ever going to slow down.* I'm betting that I'll get a lot more of their postcards from the far corners of the earth for many years to come.

CHAPTER 9

Time to Save $10,000 a Year (or MUCH More!) Now That You're Retired

----

Everybody knows the old saying "Time is money." In other words, if you're wasting time, you're wasting money. You could be using that time to apply your nose to the nearest grindstone and earn some more bucks instead.

But for us cheapskates, we think a lot more about the reverse axiom. Namely, "Money is time." As mentioned earlier, most people make most of their money by selling their time—that most finite, universal, valuable of all resources that each of us has here on earth—in exchange for cold, hard cash. Cheapskates understand this and realize that if they spend less money, they'll be able to spend less time earning money they really don't need. They understand that you can regain precious time in your life by simply spending less and consuming less. Or, as I often say, cheapskates know that time, and the stuff they can do with it, is worth more than money, and the stuff they can buy with it.

If you adopt that unique cheapskate perspective about time and money, it's likely to have a profound—and profoundly positive—impact on your life and, specifically, on your thoughts and plans concerning retirement. You're likely to place a higher priority on retiring earlier, now that you understand that time is ultimately worth more than money and stuff. And you're actually likely to be able to retire earlier than you thought, now that you understand that the spending side of personal finance is even more important than the earning side, and that the spending side is something that *you* can largely control.

There's an added bonus, too, a sort of Cheapskate's Early Retirement Dividend: the sooner you regain control of your time by retiring early, the more time you'll have to save even more. Here are some ways to make your newfound free time really pay off.

More Time to Do-It-Yourself

Will Rogers said: *Half our life is spent trying to find something to do with the time we have rushed through life trying to save.* For a lot of people, that pretty accurately describes the dichotomy between their working years and their retirement years. But for cheapskates, at least a portion of that found-time is spent on activities that can lower their cost of living even further by doing more things for themselves. At the same time these "constructive hobbies" can be a lot of fun if you approach them with a can-do positive attitude. Consider these money-saving pastimes:

• **A stitch in time saves nine ($900, that is).** "My mother always sewed and knitted, and both of my grandmothers did as well. They tried to teach me when I was a kid, but I never really got into it." Mary Bosdorf had all but forgotten about the sewing machine she inherited after her mother passed away, until she retired and rediscovered it hiding on a shelf in the attic. At first she thought about selling it or donating it to the local thrift store, but it reminded her of her mother, and the machine was top-of-the-line and still in good condition. "I started thinking about Mom and my grandmas and remembering how much joy they got from making their own clothes and sewing all kinds of things. I started feeling sad that I hadn't spent more time with them, learning about something that they loved doing." Rather than continuing to feel sorry for herself and getting rid of her mother's sewing machine, Mary resolved to learn the skill she'd turned her back on earlier in life. A couple of free basic sewing classes offered by a local fabric store got her started and led her to the American Sewing Guild (www.asg.org), a national nonprofit organization with chapters around the country that can help you "get your thread on" and become more proficient. Now sewing is one of Mary's favorite pastimes, and in the two years since she carried her mom's machine down from the attic, she estimates that she's saved over **$900** by making literally all of her own clothes, plus many other items and gifts for family and friends. Mary's newly converted sewing room (formerly one of her kids' bedrooms) prominently features photographs of her mother and grandmothers. "They keep an eye on me just to make sure I don't make any mistakes," she says with a smile.

- **Save green with your green thumb, and get in shape at the same time.** Lawn and garden care is an $80-billion-a-year industry in the United States, with the average homeowner spending about $1,100 per year on lawn care, landscaping, and gardening, with about half of that amount—roughly **$500**—being shelled out for labor alone. Not only can you save that money by doing the work yourself, but as we saw in Chapter 7, gardening and other yard work is also good exercise and burns some major calories.

- **Make more of your own gifts for friends and family members.** The average US household spends more than **$1,000** on gifts every year, according to the 2011 US Bureau of Labor Statistics' Consumer Expenditure Survey. And for some, that amount would be a bargain. "With six kids and sixteen grandkids, we were spending thousands of dollars on gifts before we retired," Marge Cline told me. Now she and her husband, Carl, make most of the gifts for their still-expanding family. "At Christmastime, the grandkids think of us as Santa and Mrs. Claus, always busy in our workshop, turning out homemade toys, clothes, you name it, for everyone on our list." "I feel more like an elf, myself," Carl adds with a wink. The website www.familycrafts.about.com is a treasure trove of ideas and instructions for home-made gifts for people of all ages.

- **Become a mean, green, DYI cleaning machine.** Okay, cleaning the house, washing the car, doing laundry, and the like may not be the most enjoyable activi-ties, but on average we spend about **$1,350** every year (per the 2011 Consumer Expenditure Survey) on related cleaning services and supplies. "Set a weekly schedule . . . get into a routine, as soon as you re-tire, when it comes to keeping on top of household chores," advises cheapskate retiree Edith Branch. She says that by keeping a weekly checklist of cleaning and other housekeeping tasks, she and her husband make quick work of household chores and rarely pay anyone for assistance. And to save more money—and the environment—by making your own eco-friendly home cleaning products, pick up a copy of *The Natu-rally Clean Home: 150 Super-Easy Herbal Formulas for Green Cleaning*, by Karyn Siegel-Maier, at your local library.

- **Simple home repairs can save simply hundreds . . . or more.** "Before Bill retired, our speed dial was packed with repairmen," Betty Wolsey says. "I'd been married to him for almost thirty-five years, and I never knew he could fix anything himself, because he was always too busy working to even try." But Bill isn't ashamed to admit that he's among what he calls the *nouveau handy.* "I didn't even own a hammer before I retired," Bill claims, although you'd never believe it from the list of home repair projects he now has under his two-hammer tool belt. "I know for a fact that we've saved *at least* **$3,000 to $5,000** every year since I retired and had the time to do more things myself . . . and it's really been fun to learn new skills." Bill honed his handyman skills by attending free workshops offered by home improvement stores, including Home Depot and Lowe's, and by volunteering to work on projects sponsored by Habitat for Humanity (www .habitat.org).

- **BYOPS ("Be Your Own Pit Stop").** Learn to change the oil, replenish other fluids, and perform routine maintenance on your own vehicle(s). These simple DIY tasks will save you at least **$100** per year in automotive service fees, and keeping your vehicle running in tip-top shape will limit major repair costs down the line and help maintain your car's resale value. The free website www.carbibles.com provides easy-to-understand visual (and even occasionally entertaining) advice for everyone from automotive novices to aspiring expert mechanics.

- **Grow your own.** You don't need to have a back forty to be able to raise some valuable cash crops to supplement your grocery budget in retirement. Even for those with a small backyard, the concept of "intensive gardening" is all about raising the most produce in the smallest-possible space. "Vertical gardening"—using trellises, cages, poles, and such to support and grow vegetables—is often combined with small "square-foot gardens," which feature raised beds (usually four-foot by four-foot squares) containing soil specifically mixed to create the optimum growing conditions. Depending on the growing season and crops planted, a single four-by-four-square-foot garden can easily produce harvests valued at **$250** or more per year. *All New Square Foot Gardening*, by Mel Bartholomew, is considered the bible of intensive gardening. Also check out (at the library, of course) *Grow Your Own Drugs*, by James Wong, for "natural remedies and beauty fixes" using herbs and other plants you can literally raise in a few flowerpots on your front porch. And if you live in an apartment or have no space for gardening whatsoever, try renting a plot for the growing season at a local community garden—they're sprouting up everywhere (find a nationwide directory at www.communitygarden.org).

☞ *You might need a Cheapskate Intervention if your definition of "homemade" is any dish that spends more than two minutes in the microwave.*

- **Bon Appe-cheap!** "I always knew I loved to eat. But it wasn't until I retired that I discovered that I also love to cook." Like a lot of people, Bob McDonald discovered what has become one of his great passions only after he retired and had the free time to follow his nose (or taste buds?). When Bob's career as an accountant was cut short by seven years due to a corporate downsizing, Bob decided to retire early, fully expecting that his equally downsized retirement budget wouldn't allow him to continue to dine on the gourmet restaurant fare he had developed a fondness for during his working years. Bob treated himself to a singles cruise to celebrate his early—albeit involuntary—retirement, and on a fluke he took one of the cooking classes offered by the ship's culinary staff. "I fell in love on that cruise, but not in the way their brochure promised," Bob says with a chuckle. In addition to taking more cooking classes (the nationwide retailer Williams-Sonoma offers some free classes in its stores), Bob has honed his chef skills with free online courses and videos like those offered at www.Epicurious.com, www.imcooked .com (kind of like a YouTube of cooking videos), www .allrecipes.com, and http://video.pbs.org/program/julia -child/. Bob estimates that he's saving at least **$2,000** a year by cooking gourmet meals at home for himself and friends rather than splurging at fancy restaurants. "Plus, I'm having a blast!"

Cheapskate Retirement Principle #17

Learning how to do as many things for yourself as possible will not only save you significant money but can also lead to enjoyable pastimes and help keep you active and fit in retirement. Plus, the accompanying sense of self-sufficiency and personal enrichment is its own reward.

Time to Capture Missed Savings Opportunities

When you're wrapped up in the workaday world, something most people don't stop and think about is what I call the "Missed Savings Opportunities Cost" of the work they're doing.

When you're retired, or even if you just have a suitably flexible work schedule, you're able to act on all types of money-saving opportunities where the key is as simple as being able to be in the right place at the right time. It often occurred to me when I was working full-time that if I factored in the value of the Missed Savings Opportunities—things

I was unable to take advantage of because of my rigid work schedule—the true net amount of the salary I was receiving would be decreased significantly, perhaps by as much as 20 percent or even more.

Consider cashing in on the following Missed Savings Opportunities now that you're the boss of your own time:

- **One-way wheels.** Many national rental car companies move much of their fleets south to Florida in the fall and then back north in late spring. If you're willing to drive one of their cars on a one-way trip within these time frames, you could pay next to nothing for the privilege. A one-way rental from Miami, Florida, to the Washington, DC, area last April cost one of my Miser Advisers only $5 per day (plus taxes). That saved him over **$160** off the normal rental rates, and that's not including the typically astronomical one-way drop-off charge, which doesn't apply to these special fleet-ferrying deals. Another—even less expensive— alternative for one-way wheels is to contact a "drive-away" car company and see if they have vehicles heading your way. Drive-away car companies like nationwide Auto Driveaway (www.autodriveaway.com) and many locally based companies (find a directory at www .movecars.com) specialize in transporting people's cars from point A to point B for them, and most rely on qualified volunteer drivers who get a free one-way trip (usually including gas money) in exchange for doing the driving.

- **Hitting the high seas on the cheap.** Just as in the rental car industry, many cruise lines need to move their fleets around the globe to accommodate seasonal markets (e.g., from Alaska to Mexico, or from New England to the Caribbean). Rather than move the ships empty, many lines offer so-called "repositioning cruises" at dirt-cheap fares. In general, you need to be able to travel in the spring or fall to find these deals, depending on the destination/routing. Check with individual lines for any repositioning cruises they may offer, or websites like www.cruisedeals.com. Of course, the cruise itself is only one-way, so you'll need to find alternative transportation back home . . . or, since you have the time, maybe you could just hang out at the destination port of call for six months and catch the same boat back on the flipside. Also, for a really laid-back experience, check out "freighter cruising" (www.freightercruises.com), where you travel along with the crew and cargo aboard commercial sailing vessels (usually in very comfortable quarters) and save a boatload of money in the process. And if you're up for an adventure and really want to stretch your sea legs for cheap, consider signing on as a volunteer crew member on a sailboat, yacht, or other vessel heading out to sea. There are plenty of crewing opportunities all around the globe, and you can find out what's available on websites like www.floatplan.com and www.crewseekers.net. Qualifications vary—from "no experience needed" on up—as do the benefits; most of the time, all "boat costs" (e.g., fuel, dockage, equipment, etc.) are paid for by the owner, and often meals are provided for crew members, although rarely is return transportation provided.

- **Let's do the bump.** During my career I always traveled a lot, and one of the big Missed Savings Opportunities I confronted on a regular basis was scrambling to catch a flight, only to have the gate attendant announce that the flight was oversold and they were giving away a free ticket or other perks to anyone willing to give up his or her seat and travel on another flight. Of course, I was always on such a tight schedule that I could rarely take advantage of such attractive offers. Now I not only jump at the chance to be bumped off a flight in exchange for a free ticket, but whenever possible I play the odds and actually *try* to get bumped. Secrets of "bump artists" like Miser Adviser Ralph Huber include flying through the busiest hubs possible, booking passage on flights that are the most likely to be oversold and on the last flight of the day to a specific destination, and increasing the odds by scheduling travel to include as many legs/changes of planes as possible. The blog *One Mile at a Time* on the website www.BoardingArea

.com provides more bump-savvy tips from blogger Ben Schlappig, who claims to have racked up over **$10,000** in free flight vouchers over a three-year period by practicing what he teaches. Score even one free domestic ticket, and that's an average savings of about **$250**. On a related topic, unfortunately, getting free or deeply discounted airline tickets by volunteering to be an air courier (someone who accompanies an important package or document to its destination for a courier service) is largely a thing of the past; with new safety regulations following 9/11 and the evolution of specialized express delivery services and technology, what few air courier gigs still exist rarely offer volunteer couriers a discounted ticket you can't match or beat on your own by shopping around.

- **Thrift store discount days and loyalty programs.** Shopping at thrift stores and consignment shops can result in big savings no matter when you shop, but many thrifts have special sale days—or even special sale "hours"—which are often during the workweek, when they're short on customers. The extra discount can be significant, commonly 25 percent off or more, although sometimes it's limited to specific types of merchandise (e.g., clothing, furniture, housewares, etc.). Check with your local stores to see if they have special sale days, and get there early if they do, as merchandise goes quickly. Even if you shop at thrift stores only a few times each year but make it a point to shop on their special sale days, you could easily save **$100** a year off their already bargain prices. And another tip for regular thrift store shoppers of any age: more and more thrift stores—including many Goodwill stores— now have shopper loyalty card programs just like other retailers, which allow you to receive discounts and other special promotions if you're a frequent shopper.

☞ *You might need a Cheapskate Intervention if you have clothes in the closet with the sales tags still on them . . . and you've already outgrown them.*

- **Ready to travel at the drop of a ticket?** "I spent my whole career as a merchant marine . . . I've been to almost every place there is. What I thought about after I retired was that I hadn't actually *seen* very many of those places." You'd expect that Justin Kurtz might be ready to settle down in his comfy little Seattle-area home once he retired, enjoying time with his grandkids and Judy, the wife he spent so much time away from while he was traversing the world's oceans. But despite his lifetime of world travels and the limited income he and Judy now live on, Justin is all the more enthusiastic about going back—with Judy this time— to many of the places he visited but never actually got to explore in his travels as a merchant marine. The key: "All those years, I was the sailor, and now

I'm the ballast. Thing is, ballast travels cheap," Justin says. He's referring to taking advantage of deeply discounted last-minute travel offers, where travel service providers are simply trying to fill seats and rooms that will otherwise remain empty. You need to be highly flexible and able to travel on a moment's notice, something the Kurtzes have down to a science, including two sets of prepacked suitcases ready and waiting in their closet (one set for warm climates, the other for cold). All the major travel websites (e.g., Orbitz, Priceline, Expedia, Travelocity, etc.) have sections devoted to last-minute deals, and an increasing number of sites like www.LastMinuteDealfinder.com and www.11thhourvacations.com specialize in nothing but "ballast travel," as Justin calls it.

Time to Be a "Volunteer with Benefits"

Volunteering for a nonprofit organization or other cause you believe in is its own reward. As Mildred Ross, one of my Miser Advisers from Michigan, who retired in her early fifties, says, "I've never been busier in my life . . . volunteering for more than a dozen groups and events. I've found that few things in life make you feel as good as doing good."

Not to diminish Mildred's altruistic sentiment, but there are also a lot of volunteer opportunities in almost every community that come with some nice perks, in addition to all the warm fuzzies. And I'm talking about more benefits than just a free T-shirt, the ubiquitous volunteer reward. (Although never turn up your nose at a free T-shirt: as Mildred told me when she showed off the colorful collection of free T's she's scored from volunteering, "If I live to be 150, I'll never need to buy another T-shirt in my life.")

Here are some volunteer opportunities that come with some pretty valuable benefits, if you have the time to pitch in:

Film festivals Most film festivals in the United States and even some in other countries—including some of the most popular, like the Sundance Film Festival in Utah and the Toronto International Film Festival—rely on hundreds or even thousands of volunteers to keep the cameras rolling. Volunteers typically get complimentary access to screenings and other special backstage events, along with all kinds of other goodies and sometimes even discounted or free lodging during the event. Requirements for the number of hours you must volunteer and qualifications vary by event. Check with the event directly regarding volunteer opportunities. By volunteering at a film festival, you can save some serious money to spend on popcorn, since passes to Sundance, for example, are priced at **$300 to $3,000**.

Music festivals I doubt that I'm the only ex-hippie who grew up in the '70s and still to this day regrets that he didn't drop everything and sign on as a roadie for Aerosmith when they passed through the Toledo Sports Arena on tour in 1975. In fact I think about it—and kick myself—whenever I hear Jackson Browne sing the official roadie anthem, "The Load-Out/Stay." But it's never too late to go back and pick up the spares you've left in life, now that you have the time. Most music festivals, including major events like the New Orleans Jazz & Heritage Festival, Lollapalooza, and South by Southwest, put volunteers to work in exchange for free admission to the event and other perks—an easy way to save **$50** or even more every day you volunteer. You can find a worldwide directory of music festivals at this groovy website, www.musicfestivaljunkies.com, and then contact the festivals directly to check for volunteer opportunities. Rock on!

National and state parks And about ten years before I wanted to be a roadie for Aerosmith, my childhood dream job was being a park ranger. I still have plenty of time to make that dream come true, too, or at least be a volunteer through the National Park Service (NPS) or many state park systems across the country. NPS has a particularly robust volunteer program, offering opportunities to do everything from building trails and guiding nature walks, to staffing information desks and designing park websites. In addition to free admission to the park, housing and reimbursement of out-of-pocket expenses may also be available—if that's the case, it could save you **$20+** a night compared to even a campsite at a national park like Yellowstone. You can search for volunteer opportunities at nearly four hundred national parks and find application materials and other information at www.nps.gov (click on "Get Involved"). Check with state parks directly concerning volunteer programs they may offer.

Theater and concerts "The added bonus is that I can sing just about any number from any musical you can name. I'm like the jukebox usher. Go ahead and pick a musical, any musical. Just try me." Years ago, Madeleine Stout, one of my retired Miser Advisers from Brooklyn, discovered a favorite pastime of cheapskates who have an interest in the theater and fine music: becoming a volunteer usher at theaters and concert halls. Those facilities that use volunteers as ushers—and a great many do—typically allow you to see the shows for free and often invite volunteers to backstage events and other special functions. In major metropolitan areas like where Madeleine lives, there are usually many volunteer ushering opportunities to choose from, but even in smaller cities and university towns you're likely to find some openings if you contact the venues directly. Over the course of the ten years Madeleine has been ushering, she estimates that's she's saved at least **$12,000** in ticket costs, something she's all too happy to sing about.

Volunteer vacations and volunteering abroad Helping people as a volunteer and seeing the world at the same time is a dream of many retirees, and there are several reputable programs and organizations that can help make that dream a reality. But be forewarned that there are also loads of outfits promising such meaningful travel experiences that are, in reality, just commercial tour operators trying to make a hefty profit off your altruistic intentions. In general, even with legitimate programs for overseas volunteering, the primary benefit volunteers receive—and one that truly can be priceless—is a chance to meet and live alongside local people in situations that aren't normally accessible to outside tourists. Some programs offer free or, more commonly, inexpensive room and board for volunteers, but rarely is transportation (other than local transportation) provided or subsidized. To search for legitimate opportunities for volunteering overseas, check out these resources: www.idealist.org, www.vaops.com, www.globeaware.org, and the excellent book *Volunteer Vacations: Short-Term Adventures That Will Benefit You and Others*, by Bill McMillon.

Sporting events As a volunteer, you're not going to score free tickets to the Super Bowl or many/any other major-league sporting events, but some minor-league and collegiate sports programs offer volunteer opportunities that can get you in the gate for free. In addition to checking directly with the team or the school's athletic program, try contacting the state or municipal sports authorities (often termed "sports corporations") where you live. These are the agencies that are responsible for attracting sporting events to your area, and many of them maintain a database of people interested in volunteering at sporting events and a listing of available volunteer positions. And there are many rewarding volunteer opportunities to get involved in through sports organizations that are part of the US Olympic program; for more information, contact the national governing body—the organization that administers the Olympic programs of various sports—for the sport(s) that interest you (see www.teamusa.org for national governing body contact information).

☞ *You might need a Cheapskate Intervention if you bought an off-road vehicle just because they installed speed bumps in the parking lot at the shopping mall.*

Conventions and conferences Even modestly priced conventions and conferences frequently charge registration fees of **$50 to $100** per day, and nowadays that's a real bargain. In many cases, volunteering a few hours of your time to help with registration and other logistics will get you a free pass to the event or at least a significant discount (and probably a free T-shirt!). Check with the organization sponsoring the conference or the professional production company managing the event in the case of bigger conventions to see if they need volunteers. Also try contacting your area convention and visitors bureau, as they frequently coordinate the placement of volunteers for events happening in the region. And on a related topic, consider becoming a Travelers Aid volunteer (www.travelersaid.org)—you know, the helpful folks who staff the hospitality desks at airports, train stations, and the like; it may not come with many tangible benefits, but if you've ever been a traveler in need of help, you know that Travelers Aid volunteers are worth their weight in lost luggage.

And those are just a few volunteer opportunities *with benefits* you can take advantage of now that you have the time. Here are some other popular websites that can help you find rewarding volunteer opportunities in your community:

www.volunteermatch.org
www.serve.gov
www.dosomething.org
www.volunteer.gov
www.1-800-volunteer.org
www.networkforgood.org
www.smartvolunteer.org
and
www.createthegood.org (a nationwide clearinghouse of
    volunteer opportunities cosponsored by AARP)

Cheapskate Retirement Principle #18

Being a good person, good family member, good friend, good neighbor, good community member, and all-around Good Samaritan not only is the best way to live, it's one of the greatest assets you can have in life, particularly in retirement. Get started being nice now, not when you need someone else's help.

AGING HAS ITS BENEFITS

Here is a list of national companies that offer some type of discount or other perks for older people (often limited to specific items or date restricted). The age requirements and other details vary—and some require AARP membership (those indicated with an * here)—so check their websites for the most up-to-date information.

DINING

Applebee's—www.applebees.com
Arby's—www.arbys.com
Burger King—www.bk.com
Chick-fil-A—www.chick-fil-a.com
Chili's—www.chilis.com
Denny's*—www.dennys.com
Goody's—www.goodysnet.com

Hardee's—www.hardees.com

IHOP—www.ihop.com

Long John Silver's—www.longjohnsilvers.com

McDonald's—www.mcdonalds.com

Shoney's—www.shoneys.com

Taco Bell—www.tacobell.com

TCBY—www.tcby.com

Wendy's—www.wendys.com

TRAVEL SERVICES

Alamo*—www.alamo.com

Amtrak—www.amtrak.com

Avis*—www.avis.com

Best Western—www.bestwestern.com

Budget Rent a Car*—www.budget.com

Choice Hotels—www.choicehotels.com

DoubleTree—www.doubletree.com

Enterprise*—www.enterprise.com

Greyhound—www.greyhound.com

Hampton Inn*—www.hamptoninn.com

Hertz*—www.hertz.com

Holiday Inn Express—www.holidayinnexpress.com

Hyatt—www.hyatt.com

La Quinta—www.laquinta.com

Marriott Hotels—www.marriott.com

Motel 6—www.motel6.com

National Car Rental—www.nationalcar.com

Norwegian Cruise Line*—www.ncl.com

Radisson—www.raddison.com

Starwood Hotels*—www.starwoodhotels.com

Wyndham Hotels—www.wyndham.com

SHOPPING, ENTERTAINMENT, AND OTHER SERVICES

AMC Theatres—www.amctheatres.com

Banana Republic—www.bananarepublic.com

Belk—www.belk.com

Goodwill Industries—www.goodwill.org

Harris Teeter—www.harristeeter.com

Jiffy Lube—www.jiffylube.com

Kellogg's*—www.kelloggs.com

Kmart—www.kmart.com

Kohl's—www.kohls.com

Kroger—www.kroger.com

Michaels*—www.michaels.com

Mrs. Fields—www.mrsfields.com

Regal Cinema—www.regmovies.com

Ross—www.rossstores.com

Stein Mart—www.steinmart.com

Supercuts—www.supercuts.com

Tanger Outlets*—www.tangeroutlets.com

Teleflora*—www.teleflora.com

Portrait by Carol Wells

VERNA OLLER

———

A Heart of Gold, and Old Zippers for Shoelaces

I never had the honor of meeting Verna Oller. But when I read about her death in 2010, I knew that we proud cheapskates had lost an important member of our tribe, a kindred spirit, and a role model for us all.

By all accounts, Verna Oller was the kind of "cheapskate" I've been telling you about in the preceding pages, someone who willingly chooses a simpler, more frugal lifestyle. Not out of greed, sacrifice, or the express desire to amass a fortune, but because living that way makes us happier and allows us to do more and share more with others.

Verna, who lived most of her life in Long Beach, Washington, a small fishing and logging town on the Pacific coast, was known for her thrifty ways. To economize, she cut her own hair, shopped exclusively at thrift stores, and once—when the shoelaces on her work boots broke—she replaced them with the zippers off a worn-out jacket instead of buying new. At night, she'd rely on the light given off by her television set for household illumination rather than waste more wattage by turning on silly lightbulbs.

"For her, it wasn't being frugal. It was just her lifestyle, and she was incredibly happy . . . joyful, really, in the life she led," Guy Glenn, Verna's longtime friend and attorney told me. "What I learned from Verna and the way she lived was that you can't think that you're giving up anything in life. If you have that perspective, then you already have everything you need or could ever want. She didn't feel like she was depriving herself of anything, unlike most of us, who always want something more. Verna found real peace and happiness in her life, as simple as it was, and that's not something that a lot of people ever find."

Working as a low-paid fish cleaner, oyster shucker, and cranberry picker most of her life, Verna never earned much money. But she was a self-taught, savvy investor, pouring over secondhand copies of the *Wall Street Journal* that friends passed along to her and spending hours at her beloved public library, studying data from *Standard & Poor's*.

Key among Verna's criteria for selecting investment firms and funds: they must have a toll-free phone number so she could call them with her questions on their dime—not hers—and they must provide postage-paid envelopes so she could send them her investment checks without having to part with a stamp of her own. And you needn't ask her opinion about "load funds" and other investments with high fees, since she monitored the operating costs of each of her investments even closer than she did her own household budget.

Between her smart—albeit rather offbeat—investing activity and her personal frugality, as far as local folks could see, Verna seemed to be getting by all right despite her outwardly spartan lifestyle.

After her husband died in 1964, Verna, who never had any children, lived on alone in the small house she and her husband had built, heating it with wood she would cut and haul herself. In her late seventies, Verna retired from her work at the fish-processing plant and simple-sized her life even further by selling her car, relying instead on the publicly provided "dial-a-ride" minibus service to get around town (at a cost of 35 cents per trip). In her nineties, she fell off a ladder while painting her house, a fall that likely knocked the wind out of her but didn't knock the spirit out of her, even for a minute.

Finally, at the age of ninety-five, Verna decided that it was time for a change. "She made the decision entirely on her own that it was time to move to a group home," Guy Glenn says. "In fact, she called up dial-a-ride and made the rounds of all of the facilities in the area to check them out for herself," finally settling on—no surprise—the least expensive option, a group home that Guy describes as "a couple of double-wides parked together" and costing about $2,500 per month, including meals. With the help of friends, Verna packed up a pair of easy chairs and a few other possessions and proudly walked out of her home for the last time.

"For Verna, moving to the group home was like going to live in the Taj Mahal," Guy says. "She was living the life of Riley, enjoying every minute of it." Among other activities, Verna developed a rigorous daily exercise program for herself and cajoled others in the home to join in with her. "Every time I went to visit her, she was doing sit-ups!" Guy says with a chuckle.

But when she was ninety-eight, Verna started suffering from intestinal problems. Although they found a doctor willing to operate on an apparent blockage, the prognosis was that she'd likely spend whatever postoperative time she had left in a nursing home.

Guy could see that Verna had made her decision. She was going to end her life just as she'd lived it—on her own terms. Verna simply stopped eating and stopped drinking fluids, and within eight days she was dead. "It was a peaceful time for her, and to see someone with so much control over themselves and their destiny was incredibly, incredibly inspiring," Guy recalls. "I think the human being hasn't really figured out what's an appropriate end of life. But I can tell you that Verna figured it out, at least for herself."

After Verna's death, Guy Glenn was finally at liberty to reveal publicly a secret that Verna had sworn him to keep for decades, for fear that—as she confided in him—"if it ever got out, it would ruin her life." At the time of her death, Verna Oller—the woman who used old zippers to replace broken shoestrings—was worth roughly $4.5 million, all of which she left to a variety of charitable causes and activities benefiting the community in which she'd lived her simple, happy life.

Rest in peace, dear Verna, just as you lived.

CHAPTER 10

How to Take It with You

So, a multimillionaire is lying on his deathbed and calls together his three closest advisers to hear his final wishes. They are, of course, his pastor, his doctor, and his lawyer.

Now, this millionaire is the kind of guy who gives cheapskates like Verna Oller—and the other generous, kindhearted, happy frugal folks we've met throughout this book—a bad name. This guy, he musters his remaining strength to tell his advisers that he, literally, wants to take his fortune with him.

He explains that upon his imminent death, each of them, as pallbearers at his funeral, will be given approximately $10 million in cash, totaling his entire $30 million fortune. He insists that each swear that he will insert the entrusted amount into his coffin before the lid is closed for the last time. "Since no one knows if I'll need it in the great beyond," he explains with his final gasp, "better to be safe rather than sorry . . ."

The advisers so swear, the old miser promptly dies, and

the agreed-upon sums of cash are given to the three men. Each inconspicuously deposits a packet into the miser's casket before it is closed following the funeral services.

A month later, the three advisers meet at, of course, a bar. After a few drinks and talking about the not-so-dearly departed millionaire miser, the pastor begins to sob in his beer.

"I have a confession to make," he says. "I thought and prayed long and hard about it. But in the end, I decided to withhold $1 million from the share of the fortune I placed in his casket to help fund the orphanage we operate, which is in dire need of funding. May God forgive me for my dishonesty."

After a pause and a sip of his wine, the doctor then speaks. "I, too, have a confession to make. As you know, our community desperately needs a free clinic where we can treat the poor and the needy who cannot afford medical treatment. So, yes, I admit that I withheld $5 million of the cash placed in my trust to support the building of a clinic. I'm not proud of my actions, but I think the end justifies the means."

Tipping back his Scotch on the rocks, the lawyer then says, "I am so disappointed in both of you gentlemen and shocked by your disloyalty. You should be ashamed of yourselves! I can assure you, I deposited in his coffin a personal check for the entire $10 million entrusted to me."

Okay, so cross "stand-up comic" off my list of possible *selfish employment* opportunities, but I'm workin' here.

What Goes Around Comes Around

-- -- -- -- --

I suppose it's only fitting—to say nothing of totally predictable—that a book about retirement should end with a short discussion about the final chapter in everyone's life: dying, death, and what happens next. No, I don't claim to have any answers about that last part. However, being a cheapskate, I'm pretty sure that if I see a blinding white light at the end of a tunnel, the first thing I'll say when I get there is, "Do we *really* need to have so many lights on?"

In a way, we've come full circle from where this book began. We're back to the same question Bob Johnson asked me in the park that day: *What do you really, really want?* If anything, that question may be even more important when considering your final wishes and estate plans, because once you're gone, there ain't no changing your mind.

Speaking of Bob Johnson, I'll make no further drama of it. Nor will I leave you wondering: my friend and mentor Bob (formally Robert B. Johnson) died of colon cancer one sunny April morning in 1988, at the way too early age of forty-one.

By that time, Bob was the executive director of the American Youth Hostels. The last communication I had with him was a message he left on the Code-A-Phone message recorder at our home, the day before he died. It was a message that seemed a little awkward and out of place for Bob, but in retrospect it was clearly prescient. Sadly, Denise and I were away at the time, and before we listened to the recording, we'd already learned through mutual friends that it was too late to call Bob back.

"Hey, Jeff, Mr. Tontogany, it's Bob. I think I finally figured it out. How to say the name of that place you're from— it's 'tahn-TAWG-ah-nee' right?" Bob's voice sounded weak, as he'd been in a steady state of decline for many months.

"I just want you to know that I appreciate everything you've been doing while I've been sick, helping to fill in at the office and all. I'm gonna beat this, you know that. But I want you to know that you're a great friend . . . I really mean that, all kidding aside. I guess maybe I've not always taken the time to tell some people in my life how much they mean to me, but I wanted to do it today, today. I wanted to do it today."

There was more to the message. But that's the part that I'll always remember and replay again and again in the Code-A-Phone in my mind.

Cheapskate Retirement Principle #19

It doesn't cost any more to create a will and make other estate plans earlier in life rather than later. But if you wait just a minute too long, not having them in place can cost your loved ones and estate dearly.

Don't Put Off Until Tomorrow What You Might Not Be Able to *Do* Tomorrow

- - - - - - - -

Getting your final affairs in order—whether it's creating a will or trust, or telling the people in your life what they really mean to you (for better or worse!)—isn't likely to be one of the most enjoyable exercises of your lifetime, but it is a necessary one. It's also one that's best done sooner rather than later. And once it's done, it'll put your mind at ease and let you get on with enjoying the rest of your life and retirement. Here are some thoughts on estate planning, the cheapskate way:

- **Wills** Obviously a last will and testament is the cornerstone of any estate plan, even though roughly 60 percent of adult Americans don't have a will of any kind, according to the legal news website www.Findlaw.com. The key points addressed in most wills are who will manage your estate once you're gone; who gets your assets and other belongings; and who will be the guardian of any minor children or disabled dependents after you die. If you die without a will, in most instances the state will make those decisions, which can come at a very high cost to your estate and beneficiaries. Even for a cheapskate, it's usually worth the few hundred dollars an attorney should charge you to draw up a will, particularly if you have a good-size estate, complicated arrangements in terms of beneficiaries, or reason to believe that someone may try to contest your will after your death. A qualified attorney (see the National Association of Estate Planners & Councils, www .naepc.org) can also provide you with other estate planning advice, which could prove extremely valuable and save you serious money in the long run. Often at least some basic estate planning advice is provided without additional charge when you hire an attorney to prepare your will. But if you have few assets and straightforward plans for your estate, then you shouldn't rule out a simple, inexpensive do-it-yourself will. Websites like www.Legalzoom.com, www.Nolo.com, and www .LegacyWriter.com walk you through the process of preparing a will (and other estate documents), and for fees averaging $40 to $100 allow you to create a will online. The document is then printed out, signed by at least two witnesses, and notarized. And at office supply stores like Staples and Office Depot, for under $10 you can usually buy a standardized, fill-in-the blank-type will and testament kit, with complete instructions for executing the documents.

☞ *You might need a Cheapskate Intervention if your plan to avoid outliving your retirement savings involves a license, a background check, and a mandatory waiting period.*

"My mother was frugal right to the end, and her will was one of those standard forms she bought for $5 at the stationery store years ago," Miser Adviser Lenore Benning told me. "We had our doubts that it was going to be legal and hold up, but we talked with an attorney friend about it after she passed, and her estate was settled between the four of us kids without a hitch. We got a little laugh out of the fact that she was saving the family money even after she was gone."

- **Durable power of attorney** There are a number of different types of "power of attorney" that apply to a variety of situations, but the most essential type is generally considered to be a "durable power of attorney." This is a document that delegates the legal authority to handle your financial affairs if you become incapacitated and unable to do so. Without a durable power of attorney document in place, no one may be able to access your bank accounts, investments, and other assets without going through lengthy legal proceedings. The above-referenced websites for preparing wills and other legal documents allow you to create a durable power of attorney online, or an attorney can draft one for you. Ideally, a durable power of attorney is created and kept in place on an ongoing basis, not simply drafted when an emergency situation arises.

- **Advance directives** This term refers to a variety of documents that allow you to legally express your desires concerning your health care should you become incapacitated or terminally ill. Common among advance directives are "living wills" and "health-care/

medical powers of attorney." A living will allows you to specify your wishes about artificial life support and other medical procedures in case at some point you are unable to communicate your wishes for yourself. A health-care/medical power of attorney is a document appointing a specific person whom you trust to make medical decisions on your behalf if you are incapacitated and unable to make the decisions on your own. Again, both types of documents can be drafted by an attorney or prepared by using the above websites.

• **Letter of instructions** This is an informal document you write yourself and can freely change at any time; no attorney or pay-as-you-go website is necessary. It isn't meant to replace a will. In fact, your will supersedes this letter. You can make multiple copies of this document, but just make sure that your loved ones know where to find a copy once you're gone, since it's likely to be the first piece of communication they will receive from you following your death. The main topics of a letter of instruction usually include the following:

    Funeral wishes Inform your survivors of your wishes and any plans you've made in advance for your funeral and the final disposition of your remains. Include a list (and contact information) of people whom you'd like notified of your death, any wishes regarding your memorial service (e.g., who should officiate, pallbearers, songs you'd like played, what you'd like to be dressed in, etc.), any details about burial plots you own or funeral services you've paid for in advance, and any special charities to which you'd like memorial donations to be directed. Also specify if you do or don't want an autopsy—and give your reasons why—so everyone understands your rationale and will hopefully honor your wishes. You might even write your own obituary (just to ensure that you go out with some good press!) and include it in the letter, or at least outline key facts, names, dates, and so forth concerning your life so that family members won't need to scramble to research those items for your obituary.

Financial logistics Make it easy for your family and estate administrator to understand your financial and legal matters and find the related documents. Use this letter to provide a summary of all bank accounts and other investments (including account numbers and contact information for the institutions), outstanding loan/debt information, contact information for any pertinent financial planners, attorneys, insurance agents, stock brokers, and so on. Also explain where you keep your important papers, including your will, deeds, birth certificate, insurance policies, Social Security statements, income tax returns, and so on. Regarding this last issue—where to store your important papers—you may want to have a safety deposit box at a bank for some valuables, documents, and backup copies, but because safety deposit boxes are sometimes sealed upon the owner's death, they can be difficult for your heirs to access. Consider investing in a good-quality home safe (one that can withstand up to 1,700 degrees in case of a fire) to store your original copies of valuable documents, and make sure a number of trusted individuals know where it is and how to open it.

Who gets my prized whoopee cushion collection While your will typically assigns ownership of your major assets and belongings to specific beneficiaries, a letter of instructions is your chance to parcel out smaller, less valuable possessions you own, particularly those with sentimental value to you or the intended recipient. This is also your chance to prevent beneficiaries from squabbling over who gets what when it comes to family heirlooms after you're gone, and to express to your loved ones how you feel about them and your wishes for their future. And if you own pets, don't forget to leave instructions for how you'd like them to be cared for after your death.

Consider making your "letter of instructions" personal and maybe even kind of fun, to lift the spirits of those you're leaving behind. Cheapskate Kevin McDonald told me about the letter he's left for his three adult children. "In my letter, I tell my kids that if, after I'm gone, they find anything around the house that makes them think I'm a dirty old man, 'all that stuff belonged to your late mother . . . she was into some kinky stuff (ha-ha)—Love, Dad.'" Actually, that's pretty good advice, Kevin, and I think I'll modify my letter of instructions accordingly.

☞ *You might need a Cheapskate Intervention if your medical power of attorney gives a panel of your ex-wives the authority to prohibit anesthesia from being administered, even during procedures like root canals and vasectomies.*

• **Trusts** The use of legal trusts is increasingly common in estate planning (in fact, overused, in this cheapskate's opinion), particularly for larger estates, where they may be helpful in reducing estate taxes and shielding assets. A "trust" is commonly defined as a legal arrangement in which an individual (the "trustor" or "grantor") gives fiduciary control of property to a person or institution (the trustee) for the benefit of the beneficiaries. You definitely need to consult a qualified attorney to know if a trust makes sense for you and your estate. Beware, though, because scam artists pushing "living trusts" are fairly common, often preying on the elderly and selling them overpriced plans and services they may not need.

Cheapskate Retirement Principle #20

How much you leave and to whom is a minor part, if that, of the legacy you leave behind. What you do with your life and the impact you have on other people and on the planet is the most important thing. Remember, assets like kindness and caring are free.

A Final Word About Funerals

According to the National Funeral Directors Association (www.nfda.org), the average funeral these days costs about $8,000, and that's not including the cost of a burial plot or headstone/marker. I may just be too cheap to ever die. Seriously, a lot of us would like to leave that amount to charity or our heirs—or spend it on more enjoyable things while we're still living—rather than fork it over to the funeral industry.

For the biggest savings on funeral expenses, consider "direct cremation" (i.e., cremation without embalming or a casket, and with no formal viewing or ceremony with the body present—a memorial service can always be held later, with the ashes present). Cremation, even if it's not "direct cremation" and you have a viewing/ceremony with the body present, is almost always a less expensive funeral option than a traditional funeral/burial. And now, at many funeral homes, you can rent a casket if you're going to have a viewing and then be cremated, rather than buy one only to have it incinerated.*

☞ *You might need a Cheapskate Intervention if, on your deathbed, you buy the most expensive casket possible just to get the frequent flyer points.*

There is also a fascinating and growing movement to attempt to sidestep the funeral industry and do without the service of "funeral directors," returning to the old-school practice of families caring for their own dead as much as possible. This includes the possibility, in some locales, of holding viewings/visitations in the family home, with the body present and without the services of a funeral director or embalming. The nonprofit Funeral Consumers Alliance (www.funerals.org), with chapters in more than one hundred cities across the country, is leading this effort. The book *Final Rights: Reclaiming the American Way of Death*, by Joshua Slocum, executive director of the Funeral Consumers Alliance, and Lisa Carlson, executive director of the

---

* Renting a casket is also a smart option if you think you might still snap out of it. The website www.cremationfinder.com is a good source of information on simple cremation options.

Funeral Ethics Organization, is an interesting and informative read.

If you still prefer a traditional funeral and burial, like most everything else in life, the costs of funeral home services, caskets/vaults, headstones, and burial plots are often negotiable, particularly if you pay for arrangements in advance and, in the case of burial plots and headstones/markers, if you buy more than one at a time. Don't be suckered in by "pre-need funeral packages," though; they're a notorious rip-off. And when it comes to negotiating the best possible price on your funeral and burial arrangements, obviously *you're in the best negotiating position while you're still in a vertical position!* In other words, don't leave the task to your grieving—and vulnerable—loved ones.

Heirs, Charity, and Your Legacy

This really, really is the bottom line when it comes to your finances and what you really, really want. Not in the sense that what assets you leave behind and to whom is the most important consideration in life, financially or otherwise. In fact, most frugal folks I've spoken with seem to consider those issues among the least important. But the legacy you leave—the lasting impact your life will have (or won't have) on the planet and on the lives of others—is truly the only way to "take it with you."

Of course, only a small part, if any, of your legacy has to do with the disposition of any assets you leave behind. The bigger portion is how you chose to lead your life, the choices you made every morning when you woke up. When you think about it, some of the people with the most enduring legacies—from Jesus Christ, Gandhi, and Mother Teresa, to Vincent van Gogh, Thomas Jefferson, and Thomas Edison—left little by way of material assets, but they profoundly and forever changed the world they left behind.

Nonetheless, selecting those individuals and institutions that will inherit your material assets is part of the process for paying it forward and, in that sense, taking it with you. When it comes to understanding the tax and other financial implications and logistics of leaving your assets to family members and other beneficiaries, I recommend the book *The Retirement Savings Time Bomb . . . and How to Defuse It*, by Ed Slott. If you're interested in leaving all or a portion of your estate to charity, the following web-based resources provide excellent information: www.charitynavigator.org, www.guidestar.org, www.plannedgiving.com. And if you're interested in what cheapskates have to say on the topic of legacy planning, here is a selection of quotes from some famous folks—cheapskates or otherwise—who I think capture the collective cheapskate wisdom on the topic:

"The perfect amount of money to leave children is enough money so that they would feel they could do anything,

but not so much that they could do nothing." —Warren Buffet

"Unless someone like you cares a whole awful lot, nothing is going to get better. It's not." —Dr. Seuss

"The willingness to share does not make one charitable; it makes one free." —Robert Brault

"Inheritance taxes are so high that the happiest mourner at a rich man's funeral is usually Uncle Sam." —Olin Miller

"While earning your daily bread, be sure to share a slice with those less fortunate." —H. Jackson Brown Jr.

"The finest inheritance you can give to a child is to allow it to make its own way, completely on its own feet." —Isadora Duncan

"It's easy to make a buck. It's a lot tougher to make a difference." —Tom Brokaw

"Never say that you know a man until you have divided an inheritance with him." —Johann Kaspar Lavater

"What we have done for ourselves alone dies with us; what we have done for others and the world remains and is immortal." —Albert Pike

"The best inheritance a parent can give his children is a few minutes of his time each day." —Orlando A. Battista

"*We make a living by what we get, but we make a life by what we give.*" —Winston Churchill

And Always Remember: *Live Every Day As If It's Your Last . . . Because One Day, You'll Be Right!*

I hope you've enjoyed and learned some things from this look at how to retire better, earlier, and happier—how to retire the cheapskate way. If nothing else, I hope it's given you a chance to think about your own life, retirement, and the remaining time you have here on earth. Maybe you've learned some lessons from the cheapskates we've met along the way about how there's a whole lot more to life and happiness—and enjoying retirement—than money. After all, once you've figured out what's truly important to you, *the money stuff really isn't that hard.*

Thank you for taking the time to read my book, and I look forward to keeping in touch and hearing any suggestions, tips, or stories you have to share. You can always contact me via my website, www.UltimateCheapskate.com, where you are now also entitled to claim the honorary title of "Miser Adviser," bestowed upon you if you so desire. Who knows, maybe our paths will cross in person some time, as they often seem to among folks who are into spending less so that we can enjoy life more.

Stay Cheap!

—JEFF YEAGER, the Ultimate Cheapskate

Acknowledgments

Retirement. On the one hand it conjures up images of a peaceful, relaxing, rewarding time in life, but on the other it can seem a little scary, stressful, and even depressing. At least that's what I thought before I wrote this book. But now, because of all the marvelous people I had the pleasure of meeting along the way, I know for sure that your retirement years can be the most kick-ass years of your entire life, if you'll only follow the examples of my cheapskate friends.

So many people helped to educate and inspire me in the writing of this book. First and foremost, of course, are all those in my worldwide network of Miser Advisers who keep me supplied with ideas, stories, and the latest trends in frugal living. You all rock my reduced-for-quick-sale world, and for that I thank you.

I owe a Costco-size debt of gratitude to the people who allowed me into their lives on an up-close-and-personal basis so that I could tell their stories in this book. Thank you Kelly and Jon Nowak, Shelle and Jonathan Cedotal, Lys and Dan Burden, Stacie Barnett, Jerry Dyson, Bruce Jackson, Wanda Adams, and Linda and Dave Allen. I also deeply appreciate attorney Guy Glenn for sharing with me the stories and background about the late Verna Oller.

I want to thank my friends at AARP for their assistance

in helping me write this book and for allowing me to pontificate regularly about all things cheap on their website, AARP.org, and in their other publications. Special thanks to Tara Coates, my wonderful editor at AARP.org, and to Jean Setzfand for her insights regarding a number of issues in this book.

There are many colleagues in the world of personal finance whom I both admire and appreciate for their helpfulness and support, including David Bach, Jean Chatzky, Michelle Singletary, Liz Pulliam Weston, Greg Karp, Vicki Robin, and Zac Bissonnette, among many others.

Without a publisher, there would be no book, and so I want to thank all of the fine folks I have the pleasure of working with at Random House, particularly my terrifically talented editor, Jenna Ciongoli, and the dynamic duo of publicity, Ellen Folan and David Drake. Thank you, Stacey Glick, my miracle-working literary agent, for continuing to find people willing to pay me for my cheap words.

And thanks to so many others for their help and inspiration, including: Carol Wells, Dorraine Darden, Bob Beard, Lester Van Der Meer, the late Ruth and Bill Nelson, the crew at Walton's Seafood (where much of this book was written), and my parents, Joyce and Doug Yeager.

Most of all I want to thank Denise, my long-suffering wife, for always loving me and believing in me, even when I'm in the midst of writing a book and I'm not particularly lovable or believable. Denise, I'm gonna love you forever, even if you do sometimes buy things that aren't on sale.

About the Author

JEFF YEAGER spent twenty-four years managing national non-profit organizations before retiring from that career at the age of forty-seven to become "selfishly employed" as a writer, public speaker, and media personality. His previous books include *The Ultimate Cheapskate's Road Map to True Riches*, *The Cheapskate Next Door*, and *Don't Throw That Away!*, all published by Random House imprints.

His website is www.UltimateCheapskate.com. and he blogs and writes regularly for www.AARP.org as the official "Savings Expert" of AARP. Jeff lives happily and frugally in Accokeek, Maryland, with his pooooor wife Denise.